C-1468   CAREER EXAMINATION SERIES

This is your
PASSBOOK for...

Senior Administrative Assistant

Test Preparation Study Guide
Questions & Answers

COPYRIGHT NOTICE

This book is SOLELY intended for, is sold ONLY to, and its use is RESTRICTED to individual, bona fide applicants or candidates who qualify by virtue of having seriously filed applications for appropriate license, certificate, professional and/or promotional advancement, higher school matriculation, scholarship, or other legitimate requirements of education and/or governmental authorities.

This book is NOT intended for use, class instruction, tutoring, training, duplication, copying, reprinting, excerption, or adaptation, etc., by:

1) Other publishers
2) Proprietors and/or Instructors of "Coaching" and/or Preparatory Courses
3) Personnel and/or Training Divisions of commercial, industrial, and governmental organizations
4) Schools, colleges, or universities and/or their departments and staffs, including teachers and other personnel
5) Testing Agencies or Bureaus
6) Study groups which seek by the purchase of a single volume to copy and/or duplicate and/or adapt this material for use by the group as a whole without having purchased individual volumes for each of the members of the group
7) Et al.

Such persons would be in violation of appropriate Federal and State statutes.

PROVISION OF LICENSING AGREEMENTS – Recognized educational, commercial, industrial, and governmental institutions and organizations, and others legitimately engaged in educational pursuits, including training, testing, and measurement activities, may address request for a licensing agreement to the copyright owners, who will determine whether, and under what conditions, including fees and charges, the materials in this book may be used them. In other words, a licensing facility exists for the legitimate use of the material in this book on other than an individual basis. However, it is asseverated and affirmed here that the material in this book CANNOT be used without the receipt of the express permission of such a licensing agreement from the Publishers. Inquiries re licensing should be addressed to the company, attention rights and permissions department.

All rights reserved, including the right of reproduction in whole or in part, in any form or by any means, electronic or mechanical, including photocopying, recording, or by any information storage and retrieval system, without permission in writing from the Publisher.

Copyright © 2025 by
National Learning Corporation

212 Michael Drive, Syosset, NY 11791
(516) 921-8888 • www.passbooks.com
E-mail: info@passbooks.com

PASSBOOK® SERIES

THE *PASSBOOK® SERIES* has been created to prepare applicants and candidates for the ultimate academic battlefield – the examination room.

At some time in our lives, each and every one of us may be required to take an examination – for validation, matriculation, admission, qualification, registration, certification, or licensure.

Based on the assumption that every applicant or candidate has met the basic formal educational standards, has taken the required number of courses, and read the necessary texts, the *PASSBOOK® SERIES* furnishes the one special preparation which may assure passing with confidence, instead of failing with insecurity. Examination questions – together with answers – are furnished as the basic vehicle for study so that the mysteries of the examination and its compounding difficulties may be eliminated or diminished by a sure method.

This book is meant to help you pass your examination provided that you qualify and are serious in your objective.

The entire field is reviewed through the huge store of content information which is succinctly presented through a provocative and challenging approach – the question-and-answer method.

A climate of success is established by furnishing the correct answers at the end of each test.

You soon learn to recognize types of questions, forms of questions, and patterns of questioning. You may even begin to anticipate expected outcomes.

You perceive that many questions are repeated or adapted so that you can gain acute insights, which may enable you to score many sure points.

You learn how to confront new questions, or types of questions, and to attack them confidently and work out the correct answers.

You note objectives and emphases, and recognize pitfalls and dangers, so that you may make positive educational adjustments.

Moreover, you are kept fully informed in relation to new concepts, methods, practices, and directions in the field.

You discover that you are actually taking the examination all the time: you are preparing for the examination by "taking" an examination, not by reading extraneous and/or supererogatory textbooks.

In short, this PASSBOOK®, used directedly, should be an important factor in helping you to pass your test.

SENIOR ADMINISTRATIVE ASSISTANT

DUTIES
Under general supervision, an employee in this class is responsible for providing various administrative services for a non-county department or jurisdiction. The incumbent supervises more than one significant specialty area of personnel, budget maintenance, office management or related functions and may supervise a clerical staff. Considerable initiative and independent judgment are used in performance of duties. Does related work as required.

EXAMPLES OF TYPICAL TASKS
Supervises the clerical operations of a large division, or of a bureau composed of two or more divisions; plans, assigns, and reviews the work of subordinates, and is generally responsible for the satisfactory completion of the clerical work performed in the division or bureau; supervises a large section, or a division composed of two or more sections, engaged in departmental administrative or management activities; plans, assigns, and reviews the work of subordinates and is immediately responsible to a top-level administrative or executive officer for the satisfactory completion of work performed in the section or division; acts as principal assistant to an administrative or executive officer generally responsible for all, or the preponderant majority, of the clerical and administrative activities of a small department, or for the supervision of an exceptionally large office, commonly styled a bureau, or equivalent, engaged in departmental administrative or management activities; performs exceptionally difficult and responsible independent, specialized administrative or management work related to accounts and budgeting, methods and organization, etc.; may represent a department in interdepartmental functions or programs, or in relations with civic groups.

SCOPE OF THE EXAMINATION
The written test will cover knowledge, skills, and/or abilities in such areas as:

1. Administration;
2. Administrative analysis;
3. Office management;
4. Office record keeping;
5. Preparing written material;
6. Supervision.

HOW TO TAKE A TEST

I. YOU MUST PASS AN EXAMINATION

A. *WHAT EVERY CANDIDATE SHOULD KNOW*

Examination applicants often ask us for help in preparing for the written test. What can I study in advance? What kinds of questions will be asked? How will the test be given? How will the papers be graded?

As an applicant for a civil service examination, you may be wondering about some of these things. Our purpose here is to suggest effective methods of advance study and to describe civil service examinations.

Your chances for success on this examination can be increased if you know how to prepare. Those "pre-examination jitters" can be reduced if you know what to expect. You can even experience an adventure in good citizenship if you know why civil service exams are given.

B. *WHY ARE CIVIL SERVICE EXAMINATIONS GIVEN?*

Civil service examinations are important to you in two ways. As a citizen, you want public jobs filled by employees who know how to do their work. As a job seeker, you want a fair chance to compete for that job on an equal footing with other candidates. The best-known means of accomplishing this two-fold goal is the competitive examination.

Exams are widely publicized throughout the nation. They may be administered for jobs in federal, state, city, municipal, town or village governments or agencies.

Any citizen may apply, with some limitations, such as the age or residence of applicants. Your experience and education may be reviewed to see whether you meet the requirements for the particular examination. When these requirements exist, they are reasonable and applied consistently to all applicants. Thus, a competitive examination may cause you some uneasiness now, but it is your privilege and safeguard.

C. *HOW ARE CIVIL SERVICE EXAMS DEVELOPED?*

Examinations are carefully written by trained technicians who are specialists in the field known as "psychological measurement," in consultation with recognized authorities in the field of work that the test will cover. These experts recommend the subject matter areas or skills to be tested; only those knowledges or skills important to your success on the job are included. The most reliable books and source materials available are used as references. Together, the experts and technicians judge the difficulty level of the questions.

Test technicians know how to phrase questions so that the problem is clearly stated. Their ethics do not permit "trick" or "catch" questions. Questions may have been tried out on sample groups, or subjected to statistical analysis, to determine their usefulness.

Written tests are often used in combination with performance tests, ratings of training and experience, and oral interviews. All of these measures combine to form the best-known means of finding the right person for the right job.

II. HOW TO PASS THE WRITTEN TEST

A. NATURE OF THE EXAMINATION

To prepare intelligently for civil service examinations, you should know how they differ from school examinations you have taken. In school you were assigned certain definite pages to read or subjects to cover. The examination questions were quite detailed and usually emphasized memory. Civil service exams, on the other hand, try to discover your present ability to perform the duties of a position, plus your potentiality to learn these duties. In other words, a civil service exam attempts to predict how successful you will be. Questions cover such a broad area that they cannot be as minute and detailed as school exam questions.

In the public service similar kinds of work, or positions, are grouped together in one "class." This process is known as *position-classification*. All the positions in a class are paid according to the salary range for that class. One class title covers all of these positions, and they are all tested by the same examination.

B. FOUR BASIC STEPS

1) Study the announcement

How, then, can you know what subjects to study? Our best answer is: "Learn as much as possible about the class of positions for which you've applied." The exam will test the knowledge, skills and abilities needed to do the work.

Your most valuable source of information about the position you want is the official exam announcement. This announcement lists the training and experience qualifications. Check these standards and apply only if you come reasonably close to meeting them.

The brief description of the position in the examination announcement offers some clues to the subjects which will be tested. Think about the job itself. Review the duties in your mind. Can you perform them, or are there some in which you are rusty? Fill in the blank spots in your preparation.

Many jurisdictions preview the written test in the exam announcement by including a section called "Knowledge and Abilities Required," "Scope of the Examination," or some similar heading. Here you will find out specifically what fields will be tested.

2) Review your own background

Once you learn in general what the position is all about, and what you need to know to do the work, ask yourself which subjects you already know fairly well and which need improvement. You may wonder whether to concentrate on improving your strong areas or on building some background in your fields of weakness. When the announcement has specified "some knowledge" or "considerable knowledge," or has used adjectives like "beginning principles of…" or "advanced … methods," you can get a clue as to the number and difficulty of questions to be asked in any given field. More questions, and hence broader coverage, would be included for those subjects which are more important in the work. Now weigh your strengths and weaknesses against the job requirements and prepare accordingly.

3) Determine the level of the position

Another way to tell how intensively you should prepare is to understand the level of the job for which you are applying. Is it the entering level? In other words, is this the position in which beginners in a field of work are hired? Or is it an intermediate or advanced level? Sometimes this is indicated by such words as "Junior" or "Senior" in the class title. Other jurisdictions use Roman numerals to designate the level – Clerk I, Clerk II, for example. The word "Supervisor" sometimes appears in the title. If the level is not indicated by the title, check the description of duties. Will you be working under very close supervision, or will you have responsibility for independent decisions in this work?

4) Choose appropriate study materials

Now that you know the subjects to be examined and the relative amount of each subject to be covered, you can choose suitable study materials. For beginning level jobs, or even advanced ones, if you have a pronounced weakness in some aspect of your training, read a modern, standard textbook in that field. Be sure it is up to date and has general coverage. Such books are normally available at your library, and the librarian will be glad to help you locate one. For entry-level positions, questions of appropriate difficulty are chosen – neither highly advanced questions, nor those too simple. Such questions require careful thought but not advanced training.

If the position for which you are applying is technical or advanced, you will read more advanced, specialized material. If you are already familiar with the basic principles of your field, elementary textbooks would waste your time. Concentrate on advanced textbooks and technical periodicals. Think through the concepts and review difficult problems in your field.

These are all general sources. You can get more ideas on your own initiative, following these leads. For example, training manuals and publications of the government agency which employs workers in your field can be useful, particularly for technical and professional positions. A letter or visit to the government department involved may result in more specific study suggestions, and certainly will provide you with a more definite idea of the exact nature of the position you are seeking.

III. KINDS OF TESTS

Tests are used for purposes other than measuring knowledge and ability to perform specified duties. For some positions, it is equally important to test ability to make adjustments to new situations or to profit from training. In others, basic mental abilities not dependent on information are essential. Questions which test these things may not appear as pertinent to the duties of the position as those which test for knowledge and information. Yet they are often highly important parts of a fair examination. For very general questions, it is almost impossible to help you direct your study efforts. What we can do is to point out some of the more common of these general abilities needed in public service positions and describe some typical questions.

1) General information

Broad, general information has been found useful for predicting job success in some kinds of work. This is tested in a variety of ways, from vocabulary lists to questions about current events. Basic background in some field of work, such as sociology or economics, may be sampled in a group of questions. Often these are principles which have become familiar to most persons through exposure rather than through formal training. It is difficult to advise you how to study for these questions; being alert to the world around you is our best suggestion.

2) Verbal ability

An example of an ability needed in many positions is verbal or language ability. Verbal ability is, in brief, the ability to use and understand words. Vocabulary and grammar tests are typical measures of this ability. Reading comprehension or paragraph interpretation questions are common in many kinds of civil service tests. You are given a paragraph of written material and asked to find its central meaning.

3) Numerical ability

Number skills can be tested by the familiar arithmetic problem, by checking paired lists of numbers to see which are alike and which are different, or by interpreting charts and graphs. In the latter test, a graph may be printed in the test booklet which you are asked to use as the basis for answering questions.

4) Observation

A popular test for law-enforcement positions is the observation test. A picture is shown to you for several minutes, then taken away. Questions about the picture test your ability to observe both details and larger elements.

5) Following directions

In many positions in the public service, the employee must be able to carry out written instructions dependably and accurately. You may be given a chart with several columns, each column listing a variety of information. The questions require you to carry out directions involving the information given in the chart.

6) Skills and aptitudes

Performance tests effectively measure some manual skills and aptitudes. When the skill is one in which you are trained, such as typing or shorthand, you can practice. These tests are often very much like those given in business school or high school courses. For many of the other skills and aptitudes, however, no short-time preparation can be made. Skills and abilities natural to you or that you have developed throughout your lifetime are being tested.

Many of the general questions just described provide all the data needed to answer the questions and ask you to use your reasoning ability to find the answers. Your best preparation for these tests, as well as for tests of facts and ideas, is to be at your physical and mental best. You, no doubt, have your own methods of getting into an exam-taking mood and keeping "in shape." The next section lists some ideas on this subject.

IV. KINDS OF QUESTIONS

Only rarely is the "essay" question, which you answer in narrative form, used in civil service tests. Civil service tests are usually of the short-answer type. Full instructions for answering these questions will be given to you at the examination. But in case this is your first experience with short-answer questions and separate answer sheets, here is what you need to know:

1) Multiple-choice Questions

Most popular of the short-answer questions is the "multiple choice" or "best answer" question. It can be used, for example, to test for factual knowledge, ability to solve problems or judgment in meeting situations found at work.

A multiple-choice question is normally one of three types—
- It can begin with an incomplete statement followed by several possible endings. You are to find the one ending which *best* completes the statement, although some of the others may not be entirely wrong.
- It can also be a complete statement in the form of a question which is answered by choosing one of the statements listed.

- It can be in the form of a problem – again you select the best answer.

Here is an example of a multiple-choice question with a discussion which should give you some clues as to the method for choosing the right answer:

When an employee has a complaint about his assignment, the action which will *best* help him overcome his difficulty is to
    A. discuss his difficulty with his coworkers
    B. take the problem to the head of the organization
    C. take the problem to the person who gave him the assignment
    D. say nothing to anyone about his complaint

In answering this question, you should study each of the choices to find which is best. Consider choice "A" – Certainly an employee may discuss his complaint with fellow employees, but no change or improvement can result, and the complaint remains unresolved. Choice "B" is a poor choice since the head of the organization probably does not know what assignment you have been given, and taking your problem to him is known as "going over the head" of the supervisor. The supervisor, or person who made the assignment, is the person who can clarify it or correct any injustice. Choice "C" is, therefore, correct. To say nothing, as in choice "D," is unwise. Supervisors have and interest in knowing the problems employees are facing, and the employee is seeking a solution to his problem.

2) True/False Questions

The "true/false" or "right/wrong" form of question is sometimes used. Here a complete statement is given. Your job is to decide whether the statement is right or wrong.

SAMPLE: A roaming cell-phone call to a nearby city costs less than a non-roaming call to a distant city.

This statement is wrong, or false, since roaming calls are more expensive.

This is not a complete list of all possible question forms, although most of the others are variations of these common types. You will always get complete directions for answering questions. Be sure you understand *how* to mark your answers – ask questions until you do.

V. RECORDING YOUR ANSWERS

Computer terminals are used more and more today for many different kinds of exams.

For an examination with very few applicants, you may be told to record your answers in the test booklet itself. Separate answer sheets are much more common. If this separate answer sheet is to be scored by machine – and this is often the case – it is highly important that you mark your answers correctly in order to get credit.

An electronic scoring machine is often used in civil service offices because of the speed with which papers can be scored. Machine-scored answer sheets must be marked with a pencil, which will be given to you. This pencil has a high graphite content which responds to the electronic scoring machine. As a matter of fact, stray dots may register as answers, so do not let your pencil rest on the answer sheet while you are pondering the correct answer. Also, if your pencil lead breaks or is otherwise defective, ask for another.

Since the answer sheet will be dropped in a slot in the scoring machine, be careful not to bend the corners or get the paper crumpled.

The answer sheet normally has five vertical columns of numbers, with 30 numbers to a column. These numbers correspond to the question numbers in your test booklet. After each number, going across the page are four or five pairs of dotted lines. These short dotted lines have small letters or numbers above them. The first two pairs may also have a "T" or "F" above the letters. This indicates that the first two pairs only are to be used if the questions are of the true-false type. If the questions are multiple choice, disregard the "T" and "F" and pay attention only to the small letters or numbers.

Answer your questions in the manner of the sample that follows:

32. The largest city in the United States is
    A. Washington, D.C.
    B. New York City
    C. Chicago
    D. Detroit
    E. San Francisco

1) Choose the answer you think is best. (New York City is the largest, so "B" is correct.)
2) Find the row of dotted lines numbered the same as the question you are answering. (Find row number 32)
3) Find the pair of dotted lines corresponding to the answer. (Find the pair of lines under the mark "B.")
4) Make a solid black mark between the dotted lines.

VI. BEFORE THE TEST

Common sense will help you find procedures to follow to get ready for an examination. Too many of us, however, overlook these sensible measures. Indeed, nervousness and fatigue have been found to be the most serious reasons why applicants fail to do their best on civil service tests. Here is a list of reminders:

- Begin your preparation early – Don't wait until the last minute to go scurrying around for books and materials or to find out what the position is all about.
- Prepare continuously – An hour a night for a week is better than an all-night cram session. This has been definitely established. What is more, a night a week for a month will return better dividends than crowding your study into a shorter period of time.
- Locate the place of the exam – You have been sent a notice telling you when and where to report for the examination. If the location is in a different town or otherwise unfamiliar to you, it would be well to inquire the best route and learn something about the building.
- Relax the night before the test – Allow your mind to rest. Do not study at all that night. Plan some mild recreation or diversion; then go to bed early and get a good night's sleep.
- Get up early enough to make a leisurely trip to the place for the test – This way unforeseen events, traffic snarls, unfamiliar buildings, etc. will not upset you.
- Dress comfortably – A written test is not a fashion show. You will be known by number and not by name, so wear something comfortable.

- Leave excess paraphernalia at home – Shopping bags and odd bundles will get in your way. You need bring only the items mentioned in the official notice you received; usually everything you need is provided. Do not bring reference books to the exam. They will only confuse those last minutes and be taken away from you when in the test room.
- Arrive somewhat ahead of time – If because of transportation schedules you must get there very early, bring a newspaper or magazine to take your mind off yourself while waiting.
- Locate the examination room – When you have found the proper room, you will be directed to the seat or part of the room where you will sit. Sometimes you are given a sheet of instructions to read while you are waiting. Do not fill out any forms until you are told to do so; just read them and be prepared.
- Relax and prepare to listen to the instructions
- If you have any physical problem that may keep you from doing your best, be sure to tell the test administrator. If you are sick or in poor health, you really cannot do your best on the exam. You can come back and take the test some other time.

VII. AT THE TEST

The day of the test is here and you have the test booklet in your hand. The temptation to get going is very strong. Caution! There is more to success than knowing the right answers. You must know how to identify your papers and understand variations in the type of short-answer question used in this particular examination. Follow these suggestions for maximum results from your efforts:

1) Cooperate with the monitor

The test administrator has a duty to create a situation in which you can be as much at ease as possible. He will give instructions, tell you when to begin, check to see that you are marking your answer sheet correctly, and so on. He is not there to guard you, although he will see that your competitors do not take unfair advantage. He wants to help you do your best.

2) Listen to all instructions

Don't jump the gun! Wait until you understand all directions. In most civil service tests you get more time than you need to answer the questions. So don't be in a hurry. Read each word of instructions until you clearly understand the meaning. Study the examples, listen to all announcements and follow directions. Ask questions if you do not understand what to do.

3) Identify your papers

Civil service exams are usually identified by number only. You will be assigned a number; you must not put your name on your test papers. Be sure to copy your number correctly. Since more than one exam may be given, copy your exact examination title.

4) Plan your time

Unless you are told that a test is a "speed" or "rate of work" test, speed itself is usually not important. Time enough to answer all the questions will be provided, but this does not mean that you have all day. An overall time limit has been set. Divide the total time (in minutes) by the number of questions to determine the approximate time you have for each question.

5) Do not linger over difficult questions

If you come across a difficult question, mark it with a paper clip (useful to have along) and come back to it when you have been through the booklet. One caution if you do this – be sure to skip a number on your answer sheet as well. Check often to be sure that you have not lost your place and that you are marking in the row numbered the same as the question you are answering.

6) Read the questions

Be sure you know what the question asks! Many capable people are unsuccessful because they failed to *read* the questions correctly.

7) Answer all questions

Unless you have been instructed that a penalty will be deducted for incorrect answers, it is better to guess than to omit a question.

8) Speed tests

It is often better NOT to guess on speed tests. It has been found that on timed tests people are tempted to spend the last few seconds before time is called in marking answers at random – without even reading them – in the hope of picking up a few extra points. To discourage this practice, the instructions may warn you that your score will be "corrected" for guessing. That is, a penalty will be applied. The incorrect answers will be deducted from the correct ones, or some other penalty formula will be used.

9) Review your answers

If you finish before time is called, go back to the questions you guessed or omitted to give them further thought. Review other answers if you have time.

10) Return your test materials

If you are ready to leave before others have finished or time is called, take ALL your materials to the monitor and leave quietly. Never take any test material with you. The monitor can discover whose papers are not complete, and taking a test booklet may be grounds for disqualification.

VIII. EXAMINATION TECHNIQUES

1) Read the general instructions carefully. These are usually printed on the first page of the exam booklet. As a rule, these instructions refer to the timing of the examination; the fact that you should not start work until the signal and must stop work at a signal, etc. If there are any *special* instructions, such as a choice of questions to be answered, make sure that you note this instruction carefully.

2) When you are ready to start work on the examination, that is as soon as the signal has been given, read the instructions to each question booklet, underline any key words or phrases, such as *least, best, outline, describe* and the like. In this way you will tend to answer as requested rather than discover on reviewing your paper that you *listed without describing*, that you selected the *worst* choice rather than the *best* choice, etc.

3) If the examination is of the objective or multiple-choice type – that is, each question will also give a series of possible answers: A, B, C or D, and you are called upon to select the best answer and write the letter next to that answer on your answer paper – it is advisable to start answering each question in turn. There may be anywhere from 50 to 100 such questions in the three or four hours allotted and you can see how much time would be taken if you read through all the questions before beginning to answer any. Furthermore, if you come across a question or group of questions which you know would be difficult to answer, it would undoubtedly affect your handling of all the other questions.

4) If the examination is of the essay type and contains but a few questions, it is a moot point as to whether you should read all the questions before starting to answer any one. Of course, if you are given a choice – say five out of seven and the like – then it is essential to read all the questions so you can eliminate the two that are most difficult. If, however, you are asked to answer all the questions, there may be danger in trying to answer the easiest one first because you may find that you will spend too much time on it. The best technique is to answer the first question, then proceed to the second, etc.

5) Time your answers. Before the exam begins, write down the time it started, then add the time allowed for the examination and write down the time it must be completed, then divide the time available somewhat as follows:
    - If 3-1/2 hours are allowed, that would be 210 minutes. If you have 80 objective-type questions, that would be an average of 2-1/2 minutes per question. Allow yourself no more than 2 minutes per question, or a total of 160 minutes, which will permit about 50 minutes to review.
    - If for the time allotment of 210 minutes there are 7 essay questions to answer, that would average about 30 minutes a question. Give yourself only 25 minutes per question so that you have about 35 minutes to review.

6) The most important instruction is to *read each question* and make sure you know what is wanted. The second most important instruction is to *time yourself properly* so that you answer every question. The third most important instruction is to *answer every question*. Guess if you have to but include something for each question. Remember that you will receive no credit for a blank and will probably receive some credit if you write something in answer to an essay question. If you guess a letter – say "B" for a multiple-choice question – you may have guessed right. If you leave a blank as an answer to a multiple-choice question, the examiners may respect your feelings but it will not add a point to your score. Some exams may penalize you for wrong answers, so in such cases *only*, you may not want to guess unless you have some basis for your answer.

7) Suggestions
    a. Objective-type questions
        1. Examine the question booklet for proper sequence of pages and questions
        2. Read all instructions carefully
        3. Skip any question which seems too difficult; return to it after all other questions have been answered
        4. Apportion your time properly; do not spend too much time on any single question or group of questions

5. Note and underline key words – *all, most, fewest, least, best, worst, same, opposite,* etc.
6. Pay particular attention to negatives
7. Note unusual option, e.g., unduly long, short, complex, different or similar in content to the body of the question
8. Observe the use of "hedging" words – *probably, may, most likely,* etc.
9. Make sure that your answer is put next to the same number as the question
10. Do not second-guess unless you have good reason to believe the second answer is definitely more correct
11. Cross out original answer if you decide another answer is more accurate; do not erase until you are ready to hand your paper in
12. Answer all questions; guess unless instructed otherwise
13. Leave time for review

  b. Essay questions
1. Read each question carefully
2. Determine exactly what is wanted. Underline key words or phrases.
3. Decide on outline or paragraph answer
4. Include many different points and elements unless asked to develop any one or two points or elements
5. Show impartiality by giving pros and cons unless directed to select one side only
6. Make and write down any assumptions you find necessary to answer the questions
7. Watch your English, grammar, punctuation and choice of words
8. Time your answers; don't crowd material

8) Answering the essay question

Most essay questions can be answered by framing the specific response around several key words or ideas. Here are a few such key words or ideas:

M's: manpower, materials, methods, money, management
P's: purpose, program, policy, plan, procedure, practice, problems, pitfalls, personnel, public relations

  a. Six basic steps in handling problems:
1. Preliminary plan and background development
2. Collect information, data and facts
3. Analyze and interpret information, data and facts
4. Analyze and develop solutions as well as make recommendations
5. Prepare report and sell recommendations
6. Install recommendations and follow up effectiveness

  b. Pitfalls to avoid
1. *Taking things for granted* – A statement of the situation does not necessarily imply that each of the elements is necessarily true; for example, a complaint may be invalid and biased so that all that can be taken for granted is that a complaint has been registered

2. *Considering only one side of a situation* – Wherever possible, indicate several alternatives and then point out the reasons you selected the best one
3. *Failing to indicate follow up* – Whenever your answer indicates action on your part, make certain that you will take proper follow-up action to see how successful your recommendations, procedures or actions turn out to be
4. *Taking too long in answering any single question* – Remember to time your answers properly

IX. AFTER THE TEST

Scoring procedures differ in detail among civil service jurisdictions although the general principles are the same. Whether the papers are hand-scored or graded by machine we have described, they are nearly always graded by number. That is, the person who marks the paper knows only the number – never the name – of the applicant. Not until all the papers have been graded will they be matched with names. If other tests, such as training and experience or oral interview ratings have been given, scores will be combined. Different parts of the examination usually have different weights. For example, the written test might count 60 percent of the final grade, and a rating of training and experience 40 percent. In many jurisdictions, veterans will have a certain number of points added to their grades.

After the final grade has been determined, the names are placed in grade order and an eligible list is established. There are various methods for resolving ties between those who get the same final grade – probably the most common is to place first the name of the person whose application was received first. Job offers are made from the eligible list in the order the names appear on it. You will be notified of your grade and your rank as soon as all these computations have been made. This will be done as rapidly as possible.

People who are found to meet the requirements in the announcement are called "eligibles." Their names are put on a list of eligible candidates. An eligible's chances of getting a job depend on how high he stands on this list and how fast agencies are filling jobs from the list.

When a job is to be filled from a list of eligibles, the agency asks for the names of people on the list of eligibles for that job. When the civil service commission receives this request, it sends to the agency the names of the three people highest on this list. Or, if the job to be filled has specialized requirements, the office sends the agency the names of the top three persons who meet these requirements from the general list.

The appointing officer makes a choice from among the three people whose names were sent to him. If the selected person accepts the appointment, the names of the others are put back on the list to be considered for future openings.

That is the rule in hiring from all kinds of eligible lists, whether they are for typist, carpenter, chemist, or something else. For every vacancy, the appointing officer has his choice of any one of the top three eligibles on the list. This explains why the person whose name is on top of the list sometimes does not get an appointment when some of the persons lower on the list do. If the appointing officer chooses the second or third eligible, the No. 1 eligible does not get a job at once, but stays on the list until he is appointed or the list is terminated.

X. HOW TO PASS THE INTERVIEW TEST

The examination for which you applied requires an oral interview test. You have already taken the written test and you are now being called for the interview test – the final part of the formal examination.

You may think that it is not possible to prepare for an interview test and that there are no procedures to follow during an interview. Our purpose is to point out some things you can do in advance that will help you and some good rules to follow and pitfalls to avoid while you are being interviewed.

What is an interview supposed to test?

The written examination is designed to test the technical knowledge and competence of the candidate; the oral is designed to evaluate intangible qualities, not readily measured otherwise, and to establish a list showing the relative fitness of each candidate – as measured against his competitors – for the position sought. Scoring is not on the basis of "right" and "wrong," but on a sliding scale of values ranging from "not passable" to "outstanding." As a matter of fact, it is possible to achieve a relatively low score without a single "incorrect" answer because of evident weakness in the qualities being measured.

Occasionally, an examination may consist entirely of an oral test – either an individual or a group oral. In such cases, information is sought concerning the technical knowledges and abilities of the candidate, since there has been no written examination for this purpose. More commonly, however, an oral test is used to supplement a written examination.

Who conducts interviews?

The composition of oral boards varies among different jurisdictions. In nearly all, a representative of the personnel department serves as chairman. One of the members of the board may be a representative of the department in which the candidate would work. In some cases, "outside experts" are used, and, frequently, a businessman or some other representative of the general public is asked to serve. Labor and management or other special groups may be represented. The aim is to secure the services of experts in the appropriate field.

However the board is composed, it is a good idea (and not at all improper or unethical) to ascertain in advance of the interview who the members are and what groups they represent. When you are introduced to them, you will have some idea of their backgrounds and interests, and at least you will not stutter and stammer over their names.

What should be done before the interview?

While knowledge about the board members is useful and takes some of the surprise element out of the interview, there is other preparation which is more substantive. It *is* possible to prepare for an oral interview – in several ways:

1) Keep a copy of your application and review it carefully before the interview

This may be the only document before the oral board, and the starting point of the interview. Know what education and experience you have listed there, and the sequence and dates of all of it. Sometimes the board will ask you to review the highlights of your experience for them; you should not have to hem and haw doing it.

2) Study the class specification and the examination announcement

Usually, the oral board has one or both of these to guide them. The qualities, characteristics or knowledges required by the position sought are stated in these documents. They offer valuable clues as to the nature of the oral interview. For example, if the job involves supervisory responsibilities, the announcement will usually indicate that knowledge of modern supervisory methods and the qualifications of the candidate as a supervisor will be tested. If so, you can expect such questions, frequently in the form of a hypothetical situation which you are expected to solve. NEVER go into an oral without knowledge of the duties and responsibilities of the job you seek.

3) Think through each qualification required

Try to visualize the kind of questions you would ask if you were a board member. How well could you answer them? Try especially to appraise your own knowledge and background in each area, *measured against the job sought*, and identify any areas in which you are weak. Be critical and realistic – do not flatter yourself.

4) Do some general reading in areas in which you feel you may be weak

For example, if the job involves supervision and your past experience has NOT, some general reading in supervisory methods and practices, particularly in the field of human relations, might be useful. Do NOT study agency procedures or detailed manuals. The oral board will be testing your understanding and capacity, not your memory.

5) Get a good night's sleep and watch your general health and mental attitude

You will want a clear head at the interview. Take care of a cold or any other minor ailment, and of course, no hangovers.

What should be done on the day of the interview?

Now comes the day of the interview itself. Give yourself plenty of time to get there. Plan to arrive somewhat ahead of the scheduled time, particularly if your appointment is in the fore part of the day. If a previous candidate fails to appear, the board might be ready for you a bit early. By early afternoon an oral board is almost invariably behind schedule if there are many candidates, and you may have to wait. Take along a book or magazine to read, or your application to review, but leave any extraneous material in the waiting room when you go in for your interview. In any event, relax and compose yourself.

The matter of dress is important. The board is forming impressions about you – from your experience, your manners, your attitude, and your appearance. Give your personal appearance careful attention. Dress your best, but not your flashiest. Choose conservative, appropriate clothing, and be sure it is immaculate. This is a business interview, and your appearance should indicate that you regard it as such. Besides, being well groomed and properly dressed will help boost your confidence.

Sooner or later, someone will call your name and escort you into the interview room. *This is it.* From here on you are on your own. It is too late for any more preparation. But remember, you asked for this opportunity to prove your fitness, and you are here because your request was granted.

What happens when you go in?

The usual sequence of events will be as follows: The clerk (who is often the board stenographer) will introduce you to the chairman of the oral board, who will introduce you to the other members of the board. Acknowledge the introductions before you sit down. Do not be surprised if you find a microphone facing you or a stenotypist sitting by. Oral interviews are usually recorded in the event of an appeal or other review.

Usually the chairman of the board will open the interview by reviewing the highlights of your education and work experience from your application – primarily for the benefit of the other members of the board, as well as to get the material into the record. Do not interrupt or comment unless there is an error or significant misinterpretation; if that is the case, do not hesitate. But do not quibble about insignificant matters. Also, he will usually ask you some question about your education, experience or your present job – partly to get you to start talking and to establish the interviewing "rapport." He may start the actual questioning, or turn it over to one of the other members. Frequently, each member undertakes the questioning on a particular area, one in which he is perhaps most competent, so you can expect each member to participate in the examination. Because time is limited, you may also expect some rather abrupt switches in the direction the questioning takes, so do not be upset by it. Normally, a board member will not pursue a single line of questioning unless he discovers a particular strength or weakness.

After each member has participated, the chairman will usually ask whether any member has any further questions, then will ask you if you have anything you wish to add. Unless you are expecting this question, it may floor you. Worse, it may start you off on an extended, extemporaneous speech. The board is not usually seeking more information. The question is principally to offer you a last opportunity to present further qualifications or to indicate that you have nothing to add. So, if you feel that a significant qualification or characteristic has been overlooked, it is proper to point it out in a sentence or so. Do not compliment the board on the thoroughness of their examination – they have been sketchy, and you know it. If you wish, merely say, "No thank you, I have nothing further to add." This is a point where you can "talk yourself out" of a good impression or fail to present an important bit of information. Remember, *you close the interview yourself.*

The chairman will then say, "That is all, Mr. _____, thank you." Do not be startled; the interview is over, and quicker than you think. Thank him, gather your belongings and take your leave. Save your sigh of relief for the other side of the door.

How to put your best foot forward

Throughout this entire process, you may feel that the board individually and collectively is trying to pierce your defenses, seek out your hidden weaknesses and embarrass and confuse you. Actually, this is not true. They are obliged to make an appraisal of your qualifications for the job you are seeking, and they want to see you in your best light. Remember, they must interview all candidates and a non-cooperative candidate may become a failure in spite of their best efforts to bring out his qualifications. Here are 15 suggestions that will help you:

1) Be natural – Keep your attitude confident, not cocky

If you are not confident that you can do the job, do not expect the board to be. Do not apologize for your weaknesses, try to bring out your strong points. The board is interested in a positive, not negative, presentation. Cockiness will antagonize any board member and make him wonder if you are covering up a weakness by a false show of strength.

2) Get comfortable, but don't lounge or sprawl

Sit erectly but not stiffly. A careless posture may lead the board to conclude that you are careless in other things, or at least that you are not impressed by the importance of the occasion. Either conclusion is natural, even if incorrect. Do not fuss with your clothing, a pencil or an ashtray. Your hands may occasionally be useful to emphasize a point; do not let them become a point of distraction.

3) Do not wisecrack or make small talk

This is a serious situation, and your attitude should show that you consider it as such. Further, the time of the board is limited – they do not want to waste it, and neither should you.

4) Do not exaggerate your experience or abilities

In the first place, from information in the application or other interviews and sources, the board may know more about you than you think. Secondly, you probably will not get away with it. An experienced board is rather adept at spotting such a situation, so do not take the chance.

5) If you know a board member, do not make a point of it, yet do not hide it

Certainly you are not fooling him, and probably not the other members of the board. Do not try to take advantage of your acquaintanceship – it will probably do you little good.

6) Do not dominate the interview

Let the board do that. They will give you the clues – do not assume that you have to do all the talking. Realize that the board has a number of questions to ask you, and do not try to take up all the interview time by showing off your extensive knowledge of the answer to the first one.

7) Be attentive

You only have 20 minutes or so, and you should keep your attention at its sharpest throughout. When a member is addressing a problem or question to you, give him your undivided attention. Address your reply principally to him, but do not exclude the other board members.

8) Do not interrupt

A board member may be stating a problem for you to analyze. He will ask you a question when the time comes. Let him state the problem, and wait for the question.

9) Make sure you understand the question

Do not try to answer until you are sure what the question is. If it is not clear, restate it in your own words or ask the board member to clarify it for you. However, do not haggle about minor elements.

10) Reply promptly but not hastily

A common entry on oral board rating sheets is "candidate responded readily," or "candidate hesitated in replies." Respond as promptly and quickly as you can, but do not jump to a hasty, ill-considered answer.

11) Do not be peremptory in your answers

A brief answer is proper – but do not fire your answer back. That is a losing game from your point of view. The board member can probably ask questions much faster than you can answer them.

12) Do not try to create the answer you think the board member wants

He is interested in what kind of mind you have and how it works – not in playing games. Furthermore, he can usually spot this practice and will actually grade you down on it.

13) Do not switch sides in your reply merely to agree with a board member

Frequently, a member will take a contrary position merely to draw you out and to see if you are willing and able to defend your point of view. Do not start a debate, yet do not surrender a good position. If a position is worth taking, it is worth defending.

14) Do not be afraid to admit an error in judgment if you are shown to be wrong

The board knows that you are forced to reply without any opportunity for careful consideration. Your answer may be demonstrably wrong. If so, admit it and get on with the interview.

15) Do not dwell at length on your present job

The opening question may relate to your present assignment. Answer the question but do not go into an extended discussion. You are being examined for a *new* job, not your present one. As a matter of fact, try to phrase ALL your answers in terms of the job for which you are being examined.

Basis of Rating

Probably you will forget most of these "do's" and "don'ts" when you walk into the oral interview room. Even remembering them all will not ensure you a passing grade. Perhaps you did not have the qualifications in the first place. But remembering them will help you to put your best foot forward, without treading on the toes of the board members.

Rumor and popular opinion to the contrary notwithstanding, an oral board wants you to make the best appearance possible. They know you are under pressure – but they also want to see how you respond to it as a guide to what your reaction would be under the pressures of the job you seek. They will be influenced by the degree of poise you display, the personal traits you show and the manner in which you respond.

ABOUT THIS BOOK

This book contains tests divided into Examination Sections. Go through each test, answering every question in the margin. We have also attached a sample answer sheet at the back of the book that can be removed and used. At the end of each test look at the answer key and check your answers. On the ones you got wrong, look at the right answer choice and learn. Do not fill in the answers first. Do not memorize the questions and answers, but understand the answer and principles involved. On your test, the questions will likely be different from the samples. Questions are changed and new ones added. If you understand these past questions you should have success with any changes that arise. Tests may consist of several types of questions. We have additional books on each subject should more study be advisable or necessary for you. Finally, the more you study, the better prepared you will be. This book is intended to be the last thing you study before you walk into the examination room. Prior study of relevant texts is also recommended. NLC publishes some of these in our Fundamental Series. Knowledge and good sense are important factors in passing your exam. Good luck also helps. So now study this Passbook, absorb the material contained within and take that knowledge into the examination. Then do your best to pass that exam.

EXAMINATION SECTION

EXAMINATION SECTION
TEST 1

DIRECTIONS: Each question or incomplete statement is followed by several suggested answers or completions. Select the one that BEST answers the question or completes the statement. *PRINT THE LETTER OF THE CORRECT ANSWER IN THE SPACE AT THE RIGHT.*

1. It is often desirable for an administrator to consult, during the planning process, the persons to be affected by those plans.
   Of the following, the MAJOR justification for such consultation is that it recognizes the
   A. fact that participating in horizontal planning is almost always more effective than participating in vertical planning
   B. principle of participation and the need for a sense of belonging as a means of decreasing resistance and developing support
   C. principle that lower-level administrators normally are more likely than higher-level administrators to emphasize longer-range goals
   D. fact that final responsibility for the approval of plans should be placed in committees not individuals

1.____

2. In evaluating performance and, if necessary, correcting what is being done to assure attainment of results according to plan, it is GENERALLY best for the administrator to do which one of the following?
   A. Make a continual effort to increase the number of written control reports prepared
   B. Thoroughly investigate in equal detail all possible deviations indicated by comparison of performance to expectation
   C. Decentralize, within an operating unit or division, the responsibility for correcting deviations
   D. Concentrate on the exceptions, or outstanding variations, from the expected results or standards

2.____

3. Generally, changes in the ways in which the supervisors and employees in an organization do things are MORE likely to be welcomed by them when the changes
   A. threaten the security of the supervisors than when they do not
   B. are inaugurated after prior change has been assimilated than when they are inaugurated before other major changes have been assimilated
   C. follow a series of failures in changes when they follow a series of successful changes
   D. are dictated by personal order rather than when they result from an application of previously established impersonal principles

3.____

1

4. For sound organization relationships, of the following, it is generally MOST desirable that
   A. authority and responsibility be segregated from each other, in order to facilitate control
   B. the authority of a manager should be commensurate with his responsibility, and vice versa
   C. authority be defined as the obligation of an individual to carry out assigned activities to the best of his or her ability
   D. clear recognition be given to the fact that delegation of authority benefits only the manager who delegates it

5. In utilizing a checklist of questions for general managerial planning, which one of the following generally is the FIRST question to be asked and answered?
   A. Where will it take place?
   B. How will it be done?
   C. Why must it be done?
   D. Who will do it?

6. Of the following, it is USUALLY best to set administrative objectives so that they are
   A. at a level that is unattainable, so that administrators will continually be strongly motivated
   B. at a level that is attainable, but requires some stretching and reaching by administrators trying to attain them
   C. stated in qualitative rather than quantitative terms whenever a choice between the two is possible
   D. stated in a general and unstructured manner, to permit each administrator maximum freedom in interpreting them

7. In selecting from among administrative alternatives, three general bases for decisions are open to the manager – experience, experimentation, and research and analysis. Of the following, the best argument AGAINST primary reliance upon experimentation as the method of evaluating administrative alternatives is that experimentation is
   A. generally the most expensive of the three techniques
   B. almost always legally prohibited in procedural matters
   C. possible only in areas where results may be easily duplicated by other experimenters at any time
   D. an approach that requires information on scientific method seldom available to administrators

8. The administrator who utilizes the techniques of operations research, linear programming and simulation in making an administrative decision should MOST appropriately be considered to be using the techniques of _____ analysis.
   A. intuitive   B. quantitative
   C. nonmathematical   D. qualitative

9. When an additional organizational level is added within a department, that department has MOST directly manifested
    A. horizontal growth
    B. horizontal shrinkage
    C. vertical growth
    D. vertical shrinkage

10. Of the following, the one which GENERALLY is the most intangible planning factor is
    A. budget dollars allocated to a function
    B. square feet of space for office use
    C. number of personnel in various clerical titles
    D. emotional impact of a proposed personnel policy among employees

11. Departmentation by function is the same as, or most similar to, departmentation by
    A. equipment
    B. clientele
    C. territory
    D. activity

12. Such verifiable factors as turnover, absenteeism or volume of grievances would generally BEST assist in measuring the effectiveness of a program to improve
    A. forms control
    B. employee morale
    C. linear programming
    D. executive creativity

13. An organization increases the number of subordinates reporting to a manager up to the point where incremental savings in costs, better communication and morale, and other factors equal incremental losses in effectiveness of control, direction and similar factors. This action MOST specifically employs the technique of
    A. role playing
    B. queuing theory
    C. marginal analysis
    D. capital standards analysis

14. The term *computer hardware* is MOST likely to refer to
    A. machines and equipment
    B. Ethernet and USB cables
    C. training manuals
    D. word processing and spreadsheet programs

15. Determining what is being accomplished, that is, evaluating the performance and, if necessary, applying corrective measures so that performance takes place according to plans is MOST appropriately called management
    A. actuating
    B. planning
    C. controlling
    D. motivating

16. Of the following, the BEST overall technique for choosing from among several alternative public programs proposed to try to achieve the same broad objective generally is _____ analysis.
    A. random-sample
    B. input
    C. cost-effectiveness
    D. output

17. When the success of a plan in achieving specific program objectives is measured against that plan's costs, the measure obtained is most directly that of the plan's
    A. pervasiveness
    B. control potential
    C. primacy
    D. efficiency

18. Generally, the degree to which an organization's planning will be coordinated varies MOST directly with the degree to which
    A. the individuals charged with executing plans are better compensated than those charged with developing and evaluating plans
    B. the individuals charged with planning understand and agree to utilize consistent planning premises
    C. a large number of position classification titles have been established for those individuals charged with organizational planning functions
    D. subordinate unit objectives are allowed to control the overall objectives of the departments of which such subordinate units are a part

19. The responsibility for specific types of decisions generally is BEST delegated to
    A. the highest organizational level at which there is an individual possessing the ability, desire, impartiality and access to relevant information needed to make these decisions
    B. the lowest organizational level at which there is an individual possessing the ability, desire, impartiality and access to relevant information needed to make these decisions
    C. a group of executives, rather than a single executive, if these decisions deal with an emergency
    D. the organizational level midway between that which will have to carry out these decisions and that which will have to authorize the resources for their implementation

20. The process of managing by objectives is MOST likely to lead to a situation in which the
    A. goal accomplishment objectives of managers tend to have a longer timespan as one goes lower down the line in an organization
    B. establishment of quantitative goals for staff positions is generally easier than the establishment of quantitative goals for line positions
    C. development of objectives requires the manager to think of the way he will accomplish given results, and of the organization, personnel and resources that he will need
    D. superiors normally develop and finally approve detailed goals for subordinates without any prior consultation with either those subordinates or with the top-level executives responsible for the longer-run objectives of the organization

21. As used with respect to decision making, the application of scientific method to the study of alternatives in a problem situation, with a view to providing a quantitative basis for arriving at an optimum solution in terms of the goals sought is MOST appropriately called
    A. simple number departmentation
    B. geographic decentralization
    C. operations research
    D. trait rating

22. Assume that a bureau head proposes that final responsibility and authority for all planning within the bureau is to be delegated to one employee who is to be paid at the level of an assistant division head in that bureau.
    Of the following, the MOST appropriate comment about this proposal is that it's
    A. *improper*, mainly because planning does not call for someone at such a high level
    B. *improper*, mainly because responsibility for a basic management function such as planning may not properly be delegated as proposed
    C. *proper*, mainly because ultimate responsibility for all bureau planning is best placed as proposed
    D. *proper*, mainly because every well-managed bureau should have a full-time planning officer

23. Of the following, the MOST important reason that participation has motivating effects is generally that it gives to the individual participating
    A. a recognition of his or her desire to feel important and to contribute to achievement of worthwhile goals
    B. an opportunity to participate in work that is beyond the scope of the class specification for his or her title
    C. a secure knowledge that his or her organization's top leadership is as efficient as possible considering all major circumstances
    D. the additional information likely to be crucial to his or her promotion

24. Of the following, the MOST essential characteristic of an effective employee suggestion system is that
    A. suggestions be submitted upward through the chain of command
    B. suggestions be acted upon promptly so that employees may be promptly informed of what happens to their submitted suggestions
    C. suggesters be required to sign their names on the material sent to the actual evaluators for evaluation
    D. suggesters receive at least 25% of the agency's savings during the first two years after their suggestions have been accepted and put into effect by the agency

25. Two organizations have the same basic objectives and the same total number of employees. The span of authority of each intermediate manager is narrower in one organization than it is in the other. It is MOST likely that the organization in which each intermediate manager has a narrower span of authority will have
    A. fewer intermediate managers
    B. more organizational levels
    C. more managers reporting to a larger number of intermediate supervisors
    D. more characteristics of a *flat* organizational structure

25.____

KEY (CORRECT ANSWERS)

1.	B	11.	D
2.	D	12.	B
3.	B	13.	C
4.	B	14.	A
5.	C	15.	C
6.	B	16.	C
7.	A	17.	D
8.	B	18.	B
9.	C	19.	B
10.	D	20.	C

21.	C
22.	B
23.	A
24.	B
25.	B

TEST 2

DIRECTIONS: Each question or incomplete statement is followed by several suggested answers or completions. Select the one that BEST answers the question or completes the statement. *PRINT THE LETTER OF THE CORRECT ANSWER IN THE SPACE AT THE RIGHT.*

1. Which one of the following BEST expresses the essence of the merit idea or system in public employment?
   A. A person's worth to the organization—the merit of his or her attributes and capacities—is the governing factor in his or her selection, assignment, pay, recognition, advancement and retention
   B. Written tests of the objective type are the only fair way to select on a merit basis from among candidates for open-competitive appointment to positions within the merit system
   C. Employees who have qualified for civil service positions shall have lifetime tenure during good behavior in those positions regardless of changes in public programs
   D. Periodic examinations with set date limits within which all persons desiring to demonstrate their merit may apply, shall be publicly advertised and held for all promotional titles

1.____

2. Of the following, the promotion selection policy generally considered MOST antithetical to the merit concept is the promotion selection policy which
   A. is based solely on objective tests of competence
   B. is based solely on seniority
   C. may require a manager to lose his or her best employee to another part of the organization
   D. permits operating managers collectively to play a significant role in promotion decisions

2.____

3. Of the following, the problems encountered by government establishments which are MOST likely to make extensive delegation of authority difficult to effectuate tend to be problems of
   A. accountability and ensuring uniform administration
   B. line and staff relationships within field offices
   C. generally employee opposition to such delegation of authority and to the subsequent record-keeping activities
   D. use of the management-by-objectives approach

3.____

4. The major decisions as to which jobs shall be created and who shall carry which responsibilities should GENERALLY be made by
   A. budgetary advisers
   B. line managers
   C. classification specialists
   D. peer-level rating committees

4.____

5. The ultimate controlling factor in structuring positions in the public service, MOST generally, should be the
   A. possibility of providing upgrading for highly productive employees
   B. collective bargaining demands initially made by established public employee unions
   C. positive motivational effects upon productivity resulting from an inverted pyramid job structure
   D. effectiveness of the structuring in serving the mission of the organization

6. Of the following, the most usual reason for unsatisfactory line-staff relationships is
   A. inept use of the abilities of staff personnel by line management
   B. the higher salaries paid to line officials
   C. excessive consultation between line officials and staff officials at the same organizational level
   D. a feeling among the staff members that only lower-level line members appreciate their work

7. Generally, an employee receiving new information from a fellow employee is MOST likely to
   A. forget the new information if it is consistent with his or her existing beliefs much more easily than he or she forgets the new information if it is inconsistent with existing beliefs
   B. accept the validity of the new information if it is consistent with his or her existing beliefs more readily than he or she accepts the validity of the new information if it is inconsistent with existing beliefs
   C. have a less accurate memory of the new information if it is consistent with his or her existing beliefs than he or she has of the new information if it is inconsistent with existing beliefs
   D. ignore the new information if it is consistent with his or her existing beliefs more often than he or she ignores the new information if it is inconsistent with existing beliefs

8. Virtually all of us use this principle in our human communications – perhaps without realizing it. In casual conversations, we are alert for cues to whether we are understood (e.g., attentive nods from the other person). Similarly, an instructor is always interested in reactions among those to whom he is giving instruction. The effective administrator is equally conscious of the need to determine his or her subordinates' reactions to what he or she is trying to communicate.
   The principle referred to in the above selection is MOST appropriately called
   A. cognitive dissonance   B. feedback
   C. negative reinforcement   D. noise transmission

9. Of the following, the PRINCIPAL function of an *ombudsman* generally is to
   A. review departmental requests for new data processing equipment so as to reduce duplication
   B. receive and investigate complaints from citizens who are displeased with the actions or non-actions of administrative officials and try to effectuate warranted remedies
   C. review proposed departmental reorganizations in order to advise the chief executive whether or not they are in accordance with the latest principles of proper management structuring
   D. presiding over courts of the judiciary convened to try *sitting* judges

   9.____

10. Of the following, the MOST valid reason for recruiting an intermediate-level administrator from outside an agency, rather than from within the agency, normally is to
    A. improve the public image of the agency as a desirable place in which to be employed
    B. reduce the number of potential administrators who must be evaluated prior to filling the position
    C. minimize the morale problems arising from frequent internal staff upgradings
    D. obtain fresh ideas and a fresh viewpoint on agency problems

    10.____

11. A MAJOR research finding regarding employee absenteeism is that
    A. absenteeism is likely to be higher on hot days
    B. male employees tend to be absent more than female employees
    C. the way an employee is treated as a definite bearing on absenteeism
    D. the distance employees have to travel is one of the most important factors in absenteeism

    11.____

12. Of the following, the supervisory behavior that is of GREATEST benefit to the organization is exhibited by supervisors who
    A. are strict with subordinates about following rules and regulations
    B. encourage subordinates to be interested in the work
    C. are willing to assist with subordinates' work on most occasions
    D. get the most done with available staff and resources

    12.____

13. The management of time is one of the critical aspects of any supervisor's performance.
    Therefore, in evaluating a subordinate from the viewpoint of how he manages time, a supervisor should rate HIGHEST the subordinate who
    A. concentrates on each task as he undertakes it
    B. performs at a standard and predictable pace under all circumstances
    C. takes shortened lunch periods when he is busy
    D. tries to do two things simultaneously

14. A MAJOR research finding regarding employee absenteeism is that
    A. absenteeism is likely to be higher on hot days
    B. male employees tend to be absent more than female employees
    C. the way an employee is treated as a definite bearing on absenteeism
    D. the distance employees have to travel is one of the most important factors in absenteeism

15. Of the following, the supervisory behavior that is of GREATEST benefit to the organization is exhibited by supervisors who
    A. are strict with subordinates about following rules and regulations
    B. encourage subordinates to be interested in the work
    C. are willing to assist with subordinates' work on most occasions
    D. get the most done with available staff and resources

16. In order to maintain a proper relationship with a worker who is assigned to staff rather than line functions, a line supervisor should
    A. accept all recommendations of the staff worker
    B. include the staff worker in the conferences called by the supervisor for his subordinates
    C. keep the staff worker informed of developments in the area of his staff assignment
    D. require that the staff worker's recommendations be communicated to the supervisor through the supervisor's own superior

17. Of the following, the GREATEST disadvantage of placing a worker in a staff position under the direct supervision of the supervisor whom he advises is the possibility that the
    A. staff worker will tend to be insubordinate because of a feeling of superiority over the supervisor
    B. staff worker will tend to give advice of the type which the supervisor wants to hear or finds acceptable
    C. supervisor will tend to be mistrustful of the advice of a worker of subordinate rank
    D. supervisor will tend to derive little benefit from the advice because to supervise properly he should know at least as much as his subordinate

18. One factor which might be given consideration in deciding upon the optimum span of control of a supervisor over his immediate subordinates is the position of the supervisor in the hierarchy of the organization.
It is generally considered proper that the number of subordinates immediately supervised by a higher, upper echelon, supervisor
    A. is unrelated to and tends to form no pattern with the number of supervised by lower level supervisors
    B. should be about the same as the number supervised by a lower level supervisor
    C. should be larger than the number supervised by a lower level supervisor
    D. should be smaller than the number supervised by a lower level supervisor

18.____

19. Assume that you are a supervisor and have been assigned to assist the head of a large agency unit. He asks you to prepare a simple, functional organization chart of the unit.
Such a chart would be USEFUL for
    A. favorably impressing members of the public with the important nature of the agency's work
    B. graphically presenting staff relationships which may indicate previously unknown duplications, overlaps, and gaps in job duties
    C. motivating all employees toward better performance because they will have a better understanding of job procedures
    D. subtly and inoffensively making known to the staff in the unit that you are now in a position of responsibility

19.____

20. In some large organizations, management's traditional means of learning about employee dissatisfaction has been in the *open door policy*.
This policy USUALLY means that
    A. management lets it be known that a management representative is generally available to discuss employees' questions, suggestions, and complaints
    B. management sets up an informal employee organization to establish a democratic procedure for orderly representation of employees
    C. employees are encouraged to attempt to resolve dissatisfactions at the lowest possible level of authority
    D. employees are provided with an address or box so that they may safely and anonymously register complaints

20.____

KEY (CORRECT ANSWERS)

1.	B	11.	A
2.	A	12.	D
3.	D	13.	A
4.	B	14.	C
5.	A	15.	D
6.	A	16.	C
7.	B	17.	B
8.	B	18.	D
9.	D	19.	B
10.	C	20.	A

EXAMINATION SECTION

TEST 1

DIRECTIONS: Each question or incomplete statement is followed by several suggested answers or completions. Select the one that BEST answers the question or completes the statement. *PRINT THE LETTER OF THE CORRECT ANSWER IN THE SPACE AT THE RIGHT.*

1. In many instances, managers deliberately set up procedures and routines that more than one department or more than one employee is required to complete and verify an entire operation or transaction.
   The MAIN reason for establishing such routines is generally to
   A. minimize the chances of gaps and deficiencies in feedback of information to management
   B. expand the individual employee's vision and concern for broader organizational objectives
   C. provide satisfaction of employees' social and egoistic needs through teamwork and horizontal communications
   D. facilitate internal control designed to prevent errors, whether intentional or accidental

   1.____

2. Committees—sometimes referred to as boards, commissions, or task forces—are widely used in government to investigate certain problems or to manage certain agencies.
   Of the following, the MOST serious limitation of the committee approach to management in government is that
   A. it reflects government's inability to delegate authority effectively to individual executives
   B. committee members do not usually have similar backgrounds, experience, and abilities
   C. it promotes horizontal communication at the expense of vertical communication
   D. the spreading out of responsibility to a committee often results in a willingness to settle for weak, compromise solutions

   2.____

3. Of the following, the BEST reason for replacing methods of committees on a staggered or partial basis rather than replacing all members simultaneously is that this practice
   A. gives representatives of different interest groups a chance to contribute their ideas
   B. encourages continuity of policy since retained members are familiar with previous actions
   C. prevents the interpersonal frictions from building up and hindering the work of the group
   D. improves the quality of the group's recommendations and decisions by stimulating development of new ideas

   3.____

4. Assume that in considering a variety of actions to take to solve a given problem, a manager decides to take no action at all.
   According to generally accepted management practice, such a decision would be
   A. *proper*, because under normal circumstances it is better to make no decision
   B. *improper*, because inaction would be rightly construed as shunning one's responsibilities
   C. *proper*, since this would be a decision which might produce more positive results than the other alternatives
   D. *improper*, since such a solution would delay corrective action and exacerbate the problem

5. Some writers in the field of management assume that when a newly promoted manager has been informed by his superior about the subordinates he is to direct and the extent of his authority, that is all that is necessary.
   However, thereafter, this new manager should realize that, for practical purposes, his authority will be effective ONLY when
   A. he accepts full responsibility for the actions of his subordinates
   B. his subordinates are motivated to carry out their assignments
   C. it derives from acceptable personal attributes rather than from his official position
   D. he exercises it in an authoritarian manner

6. A newly appointed manager is assigned to assist the head of a small developing agency handling innovative programs. Although this manager is a diligent worker, he does not delegate authority to middle- and lower-echelon supervisors.
   The MOST important reason why it would be desirable to change this attitude toward delegation is because otherwise
   A. he may have to assume more responsibility for the actions of his subordinates than is implied in the authority delegated to him
   B. his subordinates will tend to produce innovative solutions on their own
   C. the agency will become a decentralized type of organization in which he cannot maintain adequate controls
   D. he may not have time to perform other essential tasks

7. All types of organizations and all functions within them are to varying degrees affected today by the need to understand the application of computer systems to management practices.
   The one of the following purposes for which such systems would be MOST useful is to
   A. lower the costs of problem-solving by utilizing data that is already in the agency's control system correlated with new data
   B. stabilize basic patterns of the organization into long-term structures and relationships
   C. give instant solutions to complex problems
   D. affect savings in labor costs for office tasks involving non-routine complex problems

8. Compared to individual decision-making, group decision-making is burdened with the DISADVANTAGE of
    A. making snap judgments
    B. pressure to examine all relevant elements of the problem
    C. greater motivation needed to implement the decision
    D. the need to clarify problems for the group participants

9. Assume that a manager in an agency, faced with a major administrative problem, has developed a number of alternative solutions to the problem. Which of the following would be MOST effective in helping the manager make the best decision?
    A. *Experience*, because a manager can distill from the past the fundamental reasons for success or failure since the future generally duplicates the past
    B. *Experimentation*, because it is the method used in scientific inquiry and can be tried out economically in limited areas
    C. *Research analysis*, because it is generally less costly than most other methods and involves the interrelationships among the more critical factors that bear upon the goal sought
    D. *Value forecasting*, because it assigns numerical significance to the values of alternative tangible and intangible choices and indicates the degree of risk involved in each choice

10. Management information systems operate more effectively for managers than mere data tabulating systems because information systems
    A. eliminate the need for managers to tell information processors what is required
    B. are used primarily for staff rather than line functions
    C. are less expensive to operate than manual methods of data collection
    D. present and utilize data in a meaningful form

11. Project-type organizations are in widespread use today because they offer a number of advantages.
    The MOST important purpose of the project organization is to
    A. secure a higher degree of coordination than could be obtained in a conventional line structure
    B. provide an orderly way of phrasing projects in and out of organizations
    C. expedite routine administrative processes
    D. allow for rapid assessment of the status of any given project and its effect on agency productivity

12. A manager adjusts his plans for future activity by reviewing information about the performance of his subordinates.
    This is an application of the process of
    A. human factor impact
    B. coordinated response
    C. feedback communication
    D. reaction control

13. From the viewpoint of the manager in an agency, the one of the following which is the MOST constructive function of a status system or a rank system based on employee performance is that the system
    A. makes possible effective communication, thereby lessening social distances between organizational levels
    B. is helpful to employees of lesser ability because it provides them with an incentive to exceed their capacities
    C. encourages the employees to attain or exceed the goals set for them by the organization
    D. diminishes friction in assignment and work relationships of personnel

14. Some managers ask employees who have been newly hired by their agency and then assigned to their divisions or units such questions as: *What are your personal goals? What do you expect from your job? Why do you want to work for this organization?*
    For a manager to ask these questions is GENERALLY considered
    A. *inadvisable*; these questions should have been asked prior to hiring the employee
    B. *inadvisable*; the answers will arouse subjective prejudices in the manager before he sees what kind of work the employee can do
    C. *advisable*; this approach indicates to the employee that the manager is interested in him as an individual
    D. *advisable*; the manager can judge how much of a disparity exists between the employee's goals and the agency's goals

15. Assume that you have prepared a report to your superior recommending a reorganization of your staff to eliminate two levels of supervision. The total number of employees would remain the same, with the supervisors of the two eliminated levels taking on staff assignments.
    In your report, which one of the following should NOT be listed as an expected result of such a reorganization?
    A. Fewer breakdowns and distortions in communications to staff
    B. Greater need for training
    C. Broader opportunities for development of employee skills
    D. Fewer employee errors due to exercise of closer supervision and control

16. *Administration* has often been criticized as being unproductive in the sense that it seems far removed from the end products of an organization.
    According to modern management thought, this criticism, for the most part, is
    A. *invalid*, because administrators make it possible for subordinates to produce goods or services by directing coordination, and controlling their activities
    B. *valid*, because most subordinates usually do the work required to produce goods and services with only general direction from their immediate superiors
    C. *invalid*, because administrators must see to all of the details associated with the production of services
    D. *valid*, because administrators generally work behind the scenes and are mainly concerned with long-range planning

17. A manager must be able to evaluate the relative importance of his decisions and establish priorities for carrying them out.
Which one of the following factors bearing on the relative importance of making a decision would indicate to a manager that he can delegate that decision to a subordinate or give it low priority? The
    A. decision concerns a matter on which strict confidentiality must be maintained
    B. community impact of the decision is great
    C. decision can be easily changed
    D. decision commits the agency to heavy expenditure of funds

18. Suppose that you are responsible for reviewing and submitting to your superior the monthly reports from ten field auditors. Despite your repeated warnings to these auditors, most of them hand in their reports close to or after the deadline dates, so that you have no time to return them for revision and find yourself working overtime to make the necessary corrections yourself. The deadline dates for the auditors' reports and your report cannot be changed.
Of the following, the MOST probable cause for this continuing situation is that
    A. these auditors need retraining in the writing of this type of report
    B. possible disciplinary action as a result of the delay by the auditors has not been impressed upon them
    C. the auditors have had an opportunity to provide you with feedback to explain the reasons for the delays
    D. you, as the manager, have not used disciplinary measures of sufficient severity to change their behavior

19. Assume that an agency desiring to try out a *management-by-objectives* program has set down the guidelines listed below to implement this activity. Which one of these guidelines is MOST likely to present obstacles to the success of this type of program?
    A. Specific work objectives should be determined by top management for employees at all levels.
    B. Objectives should be specific, attainable, and preferably measurable as to units, costs, ratios, time, etc.
    C. Standards of performance should be either qualitative or quantitative, preferably quantitative.
    D. There should be recognition and rewards for successful achievement or objectives.

20. Of the following, the MOST meaningful way to express productivity where employees work a standard number of hours each day is in terms of the relationship between man-
    A. hours expended and number of work-units needed to produce the final product
    B. days expended and goods and services produced
    C. days and energy expended
    D. days expended and number of workers

21. Agencies often develop productivity indices for many of their activities. 21._____
Of the following, the MOST important use for such indices is generally to
    A. measure the agency's output against its own performance
    B. improve quality standards while letting productivity remain unchanged
    C. compare outputs of the agency with outputs in private industry
    D. determine manpower requirements

22. The MOST outstanding characteristic of staff authority, such as that of a public 22._____
relations officer in an agency, as compared with line authority, is generally
accepted to be
    A. reliance upon personal attributes
    B. direct relationship to the primary objectives of the organization
    C. absence of the right to direct or command
    D. responsibility for attention to technical details

23. In the traditional organization structure, there are often more barriers to 23._____
upward communication than to downward communication.
From the viewpoint of a manager whose goal is to overcome obstacles to
communication, this situation should be
    A. *accepted*; the downward system is the more important since it is highly
       directive, giving necessary orders, instructions, and procedures
    B. *changed*; the upward system should receive more emphasis than the
       downward system, which represents stifling bureaucratic authority
    C. *accepted*; it is generally conceded that upward systems supply enough
       feedback for control purposes necessary to the organization's survival
    D. *changed*; research has generally verified the need for an increase in
       upward communications to supply more information about employees'
       ideas, attitudes, and performance

24. A principal difficulty in productivity measurement for local government services 24._____
is in defining and measuring output, a problem familiar to managers. A
measurement that merely looks good, but which may be against the public
interest, is another serious problem. Managers should avoid encouraging
employees to take actions that lead to such measurements.
In accordance with the foregoing statement, it would be MOST desirable for a
manager to develop a productivity measure that
    A. correlates the actual productivity measure with impact on benefit to the
       citizenry
    B. does not allow for a mandated annual increase in productivity
    C. firmly fixes priorities for resource allocations
    D. uses numerical output, by itself, in productivity incentive plans

25. For a manager, the MOST significant finding of the Hawthorne studies and 25._____
experiments is that an employee's productivity is affected MOST favorably
when the
    A. importance of tasks is emphasized and there is a logical arrangement of
       work functions

B. physical surroundings and work conditions are improved
C. organization has a good public relations program
D. employee is given recognition and allowed to participate in decision-making

---

KEY (CORRECT ANSWERS)

1.	D	11.	A
2.	D	12.	C
3.	B	13.	C
4.	C	14.	A
5.	B	15.	D
6.	D	16.	A
7.	A	17.	C
8.	D	18.	D
9.	C	19.	A
10.	D	20.	B

21.	A
22.	C
23.	D
24.	A
25.	D

TEST 2

DIRECTIONS: Each question or incomplete statement is followed by several suggested answers or completions. Select the one that BEST answers the question or completes the statement. *PRINT THE LETTER OF THE CORRECT ANSWER IN THE SPACE AT THE RIGHT.*

1. Which one of the following is generally accepted by managers as the MOST difficult aspect of a training program in staff supervision?
   A. Determining training needs of the staff
   B. Evaluating the effectiveness of the courses
   C. Locating capable instructors to teach the courses
   D. Finding adequate space and scheduling acceptable times for all participants

   1.____

2. Assume that, as a manager, you have decided to start a job enrichment program with the purpose of making jobs more varied and interesting in an effort to increase the motivation of a certain group of workers in your division.
   Which one of the following should generally NOT be part of this program?
   A. Increasing the accountability of these individuals for their own work
   B. Granting additional authority or job freedom to these employees in their job activities
   C. Mandating increased monthly production goals for this group of employees
   D. Giving each of these employees a complete unit of work

   2.____

3. Both employer and employee have an important stake in effective preparation for retirement.
   According to modern management thinking, the one of the following which is probably the MOST important aspect of a sound pre-retirement program is to
   A. make assignments that utilize the employee's abilities fully
   B. reassign the employee to a less demanding position in the organization for the last year or two he is on the job
   C. provide the employee with financial data and other facts that would be pertinent to his retirement planning
   D. encourage the employee to develop interests and hobbies which are connected with the job

   3.____

4. The civil service system generally emphasizes a policy of *promotion-from-within*. Employees in the direct line of promotion in a given occupational group are eligible for promotion to the next higher title in that occupational group.
   Which one of the following is LEAST likely to occur as a result of this policy and practice?
   A. Training time will be saved since employees in higher-level positions are already familiar with many agency rules, regulations, and procedures.
   B. The recruitment section will be able to show prospective employees that there are distinct promotional opportunities.

   4.____

C. Employees will be provided with a clear-cut picture as to their possible career ladder.
D. Employees will be encouraged to seek broad-based training and education to enhance their promotability.

5. From a management point of view, the MAIAN drawback of seniority as opposed to merit as a basis for granting pay increases to workers is that a pay increase system based on seniority
   A. is favored by unions
   B. upsets organizational status relationships
   C. may encourage mediocre performance by employees
   D. is more difficult to administer than a merit plan

5._____

6. One of the actions that is often taken against employees in the non-uniformed forces who are accused of misconduct on the job is suspension without pay. The MOST justifiable reason for taking such action is to
   A. ease an employee out of the agency
   B. enable an investigation to be conducted into the circumstances of the offense
   C. improve the performance of the employee when he returns to the job
   D. punish the employee by imposing a hardship on him

6._____

7. A manager has had difficulty in getting good clerical employees to staff a filing section under his supervision. To add to his problems, one of his most competent senior clerks requests a transfer to the accounting division so that he can utilize his new accounting skill, which he is acquiring by going to college at night. The manager attempts to keep the senior clerk in his filing section by calling the director of personnel and getting him to promise not to authorize any transfer.
GENERALLY, this manager's action is
   A. *desirable*; he should not help his staff to develop themselves if it means losing good people
   B. *undesirable*; he should recommend that the senior clerk get a raise in the hope of preventing him from transferring to another section
   C. *desirable*; it shows that the manager is concerned about the senior clerk's future performance
   D. *undesirable*; it is good policy to transfer employees to the type of work they are interested in and for which they are acquiring training

7._____

8. One of your subordinates, a unit supervisor, comes to you, the division chief, because he feels that he is working out of title, and he suggests that his competitive class position should be reclassified to a higher title.
Which one of the following statements that the subordinate has made is generally LEAST likely to be a valid support for his suggestion?
   A. The work he is doing conforms to the general statement of duties and responsibilities as described in the class specification for the next higher title in his occupational group.
   B. Most of the typical tasks he performs are listed in the class specification for a title with a higher salary range and are not listed for his current title.

8.

3 (#2)

C. His education and experience qualifications far exceed the minimum requirements for the position he holds.
D. His duties and responsibilities have changed recently and are now similar to those of his supervisor.

9. Assume that a class specification for a competitive title used exclusively by your agency is outdated, and that no examination for the title has been given since the specification was issued.
   Of the following, the MOST appropriate action for your agency to take is to
   A. make the necessary changes and submit the revised class specification to the city civil service commission
   B. write the personnel director to recommend that the class specification be updated, giving the reasons and suggested revisions
   C. prepare a revised class specification and submit it to the office of management and budget for their approval
   D. secure approval of the state civil service commission to update the class specification, and then submit the revised specification to the city civil service commission

9._____

10. Assume that an appropriate eligible list has been established and certified to your agency for a title in which a large number of provisionals are serving in your agency.
    In order to obtain permission from the personnel director to retain some of them beyond the usual time limit set by rules (two months) following certification of the list, which one of the following conditions MUST apply?
    A. The positions are sensitive and require investigation of eligibles prior to appointment.
    B. Replacement of all provisionals within two months would impair essential public service.
    C. Employees are required to work rotating shifts, including nights and weekends.
    D. The duties of the positions require unusual physical effort and endurance.

10._____

11. Under the federally-funded Comprehensive Employment and Training Act (CETA), the hiring by the city of non-civil servants for CETA jobs is PROHIBITED when the
    A. applicants are unemployed because of seasonal lay-offs in private industry
    B. applicants do not meet U.S. citizenship and city residence requirements
    C. jobs have minimum requirements of specialized professional or technical training and experience
    D. jobs are comparable to those performed by laid-off civil servants

11._____

12. Assume you are in charge of the duplicating service in your agency. Since employees assigned to this operation lack a sense of accomplishment because the work is highly specialized and repetitive, your superior proposes to enlarge the jobs of these workers and asks you about your reaction to this strategy.

12._____

The MOST appropriate response for you to make is that job enlargement would be
- A. *undesirable*, primarily because it would increase production costs
- B. *undesirable*, primarily because it would diminish the quality of the output
- C. *desirable*, primarily because it might make it possible to add an entire level of management to the organizational structure of your agency
- D. *desirable*, primarily because it might make it possible to decrease the amount of supervision the workers will require

13. According to civil service law, layoff or demotion must be made in inverse order of seniority among employees permanently serving in the same title and layoff unit.
Which one of the following is now the CORRECT formula for computing seniority?
Total continuous service in the
    - A. competitive class only
    - B. competitive, non-competitive, or labor class
    - C. classified or unclassified services
    - D. competitive, non-competitive, exempt, and labor classes

14. Under which of the following conditions would an appointing officer be permitted to consider the sex of a candidate in making an employment decision?
When
    - A. the duties of the position require considerable physical effort or strength
    - B. the duties of the position are considered inherently dangerous
    - C. separate toilet facilities and dressing rooms for the sexes are unavailable and/or cannot be provided in any event
    - D. the public has indicated a preference to be served by persons of a specified sex

15. Assume that an accountant under your supervision signs out to the field to make an agency audit. It is later discovered that, although he had reported himself at work until 5 P.M. that day, he had actually left for home at 3:30 P.M. Although this accountant has worked for the city for ten years and has had an excellent performance record, he is demoted to a lower title in punishment for this breach of duty.
According to generally accepted thinking on personnel management, the disciplinary action taken in this case should be considered
    - A. *appropriate*; a lesser penalty might encourage repetition of the offense
    - B. *inappropriate*; the correct penalty for such a breach of duty should be dismissal
    - C. *appropriate*; the accountant's abilities may be utilized better in the new assignment
    - D. *inappropriate*; the impact of a continuing stigma and loss of salary is not commensurate with the offense committed

16. Line managers often request more funds for their units than are actually required to attain their current objectives.
Which one of the following is the MOST important reason for such inflated budget requests?
The
    A. expectation that budget examiners will exercise their prerogative of budget cutting
    B. line manager's interest in improving the performance of his unit is thereby indicated to top management
    C. expectation that such requests will make it easier to obtain additional funds in future years
    D. opinion that it makes sense to obtain additional funds and decide later how to use them

16._____

17. Integrating budgeting with program planning and evaluation in a city agency is GENERALLY considered to be
    A. *undesirable*; budgeting must focus on the fiscal year at hand, whereas planning must concern itself with developments over a period of years
    B. *desirable*; budgeting facilitates the choice-making process by evaluating the financial implications of agency programs and forcing cost comparisons among them
    C. *undesirable*; accountants and statisticians with the required budgetary skills have little familiarity with the substantive programs that the agency is conducting
    D. *desirable*; such a partnership increases the budgetary skills of planners, thus promoting more effective use of public resources

17._____

18. An aspect of the managerial function, a budget is described BEST as a
    A. set of qualitative management controls over productivity
    B. tool based on historical accounting reports
    C. type of management plan expressed in quantitative terms
    D. precise estimate of future quantitative and qualitative contingencies

18._____

19. Which one of the following is generally accepted as the MAJOR immediate advantage of installing a system of program budgeting?
It
    A. encourages managers to relate their decisions to the agency's long-range goals
    B. is a replacement for the financial or fiscal budget
    C. decreases the need for managers to make trade-offs in the decision-making process
    D. helps to adjust budget figures to provide for unexpected developments

19._____

20. Of the following, the BEST means for assuring necessary responsiveness of a budgetary program to changing conditions is by
    A. overestimating budgetary expenditures by 15% and assigning the excess to unforeseen problem areas
    B. underestimating budgetary expenditures by at least 20% and setting aside a reserve account in the same amount

20._____

C. reviewing and revising the budget at regular intervals so that it retains its character as a current document
D. establishing *budget-by-exception* policies for each division in the agency

21. According to expert thought in the area of budgeting, participation in the preparation of a government agency's budget should GENERALLY involve
    A. only top management
    B. only lower levels of management
    C. all levels of the organization
    D. only a central budget office or bureau

    21.____

22. Of the following, the MOST useful guide to analysis of budget estimates for the coming fiscal year is a comparison with
    A. appropriations as amended for the current fiscal year
    B. manpower requirements for the previous two years
    C. initial appropriations for the current fiscal year
    D. budget estimates for the preceding five years

    22.____

23. A manager assigned to analyze the costs and benefits associated with a program which the agency head proposes to undertake may encounter certain factors which cannot be measured in dollar terms.
    In such a case, the manager should GENERALLY
    A. ignore the factors which cannot be quantified
    B. evaluate the factors in accordance with their degree of importance to the overall agency goals
    C. give the factors weight equal to the weight given to measurable costs and benefits
    D. assume that non-measurable costs and benefits will balance out against one another

    23.____

24. If city employees believe that they are receiving adverse treatment in terms of training and disciplinary actions because of their national origin, they may file charges of discrimination with the Federal government's
    A. Human Rights Commission
    B. Public Employee Relations Board
    C. Equal Employment Opportunity Commission
    D. United States Department of Commerce

    24.____

25. Under existing employment statutes, the city is obligated, as an employer, to take *affirmative action* in certain instances.
    This requirement has been imposed to ensure that
    A. employees who are members of minority groups, or women, be given special opportunities for training and promotion even though they are not available to other employees
    B. employees or applicants for employment are treated without regard to race, color, religion, sex, or national origin

    25.____

C. proof exists to show that the city has acted with good intentions in any case where it has disregarded this requirement
D. men and women are treated alike except where State law provides special hour or working conditions for women

KEY (CORRECT ANSWERS)

1.	B		11.	D
2.	C		12.	D
3.	C		13.	D
4.	D		14.	C
5.	C		15.	D
6.	B		16.	A
7.	D		17.	B
8.	C		18.	C
9.	B		19.	A
10.	B		20.	D

21.	C
22.	A
23.	B
24.	C
25.	B

EXAMINATION SECTION
TEST 1

DIRECTIONS: Each question or incomplete statement is followed by several suggested answers or completions. Select the one that BEST answers the question or completes the statement. *PRINT THE LETTER OF THE CORRECT ANSWER IN THE SPACE AT THE RIGHT.*

1. Assume that a civil service list has been established for a position in an agency which had provisional appointees serving in three permanent vacancies. One of these provisionals is on the eligible list, but was discharged because permanent appointments were accepted by three eligibles who were higher on the list. The former provisional has complained to the agency head, alleging that special efforts were made to appoint these eligible. The personnel officer of the agency should advise the agency head that
   A. the court could compel them to appoint the former provisional appointee
   B. he is required by civil service law to appoint the higher ranking eligibles from the list
   C. the human rights commission could compel him to appoint the former provisional appointee
   D. he should attempt conciliation

2. Assume that two accountants working in a section under your supervision were appointed from the same eligible list. Accountant Jones received a higher score on the competitive examination than Accountant Doe; Jones was third on the eligible list and Doe was fifth. Jones was told to report to work on March 15 but Doe, who was working under a provisional appointment, was given permanent status as of March 1. For economic reasons, your agency head is considering abolishing one position of accountant and requests guidance from you before making any decision.
It would be BEST to tell him that
   A. if he decides to abolish one position of accountant, he should lay off Jones because Doe was given permanent status before Jones
   B. under the rule of *one in three*, Doe could not have been reached for appointment before Jones, so that Doe would have to be laid off first
   C. if he decides to abolish one position of accountant, he should lay off Doe because Doe's provisional appointment was in violation of the Civil Service Law
   D. he should evaluate the performance of Jones and Doe before making any determination as to which accountant to lay off

3. An employee who has been on the job for a number of years became a problem drinker during the past year. The supervisor and this employee are good friends.
Because this problem has been affecting the work of the unit adversely, it would be BEST for the supervisor to

A. attempt to cover up the problem by moving the subordinate's desk to a corner of the office where he would not be noticed so readily
B. refer the employee for counseling to the employee counseling service
C. reassign some of the problem drinker's responsibilities to other employees
D. send the employee home in a tactful manner whenever he reports for duty in an unfit condition

4. In a strike situation, a member of the striking union reports for work but abstains from the full performance of his duties in his normal manner. According to the state civil service law, it is ACCURATE to say that the
   A. employee should be presumed to have engaged in a strike
   B. employee should not be presumed to have engaged in a strike
   C. city must bear the burden of proving that the employee engaged in a strike
   D. city may deny the employee the opportunity to rebut any charge that he engaged in a strike

5. Assume that, as a manager in a health agency which is establishing a *management-by-objective* program, you are asked to review and make recommendations on the following goals set by the agency head for the coming year.
   Which one of these objectives should you recommend dropping because of difficulty in verifying the degree to which the goal has been attained?
   A. Establishing night clinics in two preventive health care centers
   B. Informing more people of available health services
   C. Preparing a training manual for data-processing personnel
   D. Producing a 4-page health news bulletin to be distributed monthly to employees

6. The MAIN purpose of the *management-by-objectives* system is to
   A. develop a method of appraising the performance of managerial employees against verifiable objectives rather than against subjective appraisals and personal supervision
   B. decentralize managerial decision-making more effectively by setting goals for personnel all the way down to each first-line supervisor as well as to staff people
   C. increase managerial accountability and improve managerial effectiveness
   D. enable top level managerial employees to impose quantitative goals which will focus attention on the relevant trends that may affect the future

7. Certain city and state employees are on one year's probation for violating the strike provisions of the state civil service law.
   According to a ruling by the state attorney general, in the event of layoffs during their year of probation, the status of these employees should be considered
   A. *permanent*, with retention rights based on original date of appointment
   B. *probationary*, subject to layoff before permanent employees

C. *permanent*, to be credited with one year less service than indicated by the original date of appointment
D. *probationary*, subject to layoff before other employees in the layoff unit except for those with one year's seniority

8. Assume that, as a senior supervisor conducting a training course for a group of newly assigned first-line supervisors, you emphasize that an effective supervisor should encourage employee suggestions. One member of the group dissents, asserting that many employees come up with worthless, time-wasting ideas.
The one of the following which would be the MOST appropriate response for you to make is that
   A. the supervisor's attitude is wrong, because no suggestion is entirely without merit
   B. the supervisor must remember that encouragement of employee suggestions is the major part of any employee development program
   C. even if a suggestion seems worthless, the participation of the employee helps to increase his identification with the agency
   D. even if a suggestion seems worthless, the supervisor may be able to save it for future use

9. The *grapevine* is an informal channel of communication which exists among employees in an organization as a natural result of their social interaction, and their desire to be kept posted on the latest information. Some information transmitted through the grapevine is truth, some half-truth, and some just rumor.
Which one of the following would be the MOST appropriate attitude for a member of a management team to have about the grapevine?
   A. The grapevine often carries false, malicious, and uncontrollable rumors and management should try to stamp it out by improving official channels of communication.
   B. There are more important problems; normally only a small percentage of employees are interested in information transmitted through the grapevine.
   C. The grapevine can give management insight into what employees think and feel and can help to supplement the formal communication systems.
   D. The grapevine gives employees a harmless outlet for their imagination and an opportunity to relieve their fears and tensions in the form of rumors.

10. Although there are no formal performance appraisal mechanisms for non-managerial employees, managers nevertheless make informal appraisals because some method is needed to measure progress and to let employees know how they are doing.
The MOST import recent trend in making performance appraisals is toward judging the employee primarily on the extent to which he has
   A. tried to perform his assigned tasks
   B. demonstrated personal traits which are accepted as necessary to do the job satisfactorily

C. accomplished the objectives set for his job
D. followed the procedures established for the job

11. The proof of a successful human relations program in an organization is the morale crises that never happen.
    Of the following, the implication for managers that follows MOST directly from this statement is that they should
    A. review and initiate revisions in all organization policies which may have an adverse effect on employee morale
    B. place more emphasis on ability to anticipate and prevent morale problems than on ability to resolve an actual crisis
    C. see that first-line supervisors work fairly and understandingly with employees
    D. avoid morale crises at all costs, since even the best resolution leaves scar, suspicions, and animosities

12. Suppose that you are conducting a conference on a specific problem. One employee makes a suggestion which you think is highly impractical.
    Of the following, the way for you to respond to this suggestion is FIRST to
    A. be frank and tell the employee that his solution is wrong
    B. ask the employee in what way his suggestion will solve the problem under discussion
    C. refrain from any comment on it, and ask the group whether they have any other solutions to offer
    D. ask another participant to point out what is wrong with the suggestion

13. Suppose that a manager notices continuing deterioration in the work, conduct, and interpersonal relationships of one of his immediate subordinates, indicating that this employee has more than a minor emotional problem. Although the manager has made an attempt to help this employee by talking over his problems with him on several occasions, the employee has shown little improvement.
    Of the following, generally the MOST constructive action for the manager to take at this point would be to
    A. continue to be supportive by sympathetic listening and counseling
    B. show tolerance toward the performance of the disturbed employee
    C. discuss the employee's deteriorating condition with him and suggest that he seek professional help
    D. consider whether the need of this employee and the agency would be best served by his transfer to another division

14. A manager has a problem involving conflict between two employees concerning a method of performing a work assignment. He does not know the reasons for this conflict.
    The MOST valuable communications method he can use to aid him in resolving the problem is
    A. a formal hearing for each employee
    B. a staff meeting

C. disciplinary memoranda
D. an informal interview with each employee

15. As a training technique, role-playing is generally considered to be MOST successful when it results in
    A. uncovering the underlying causes of conflict so that any recurrences are prevented
    B. recreating an actual work situation which involves conflict among people and in which members of the group simulate specific personalities
    C. freeing some people from patterns of rigid thinking and enabling them to look at themselves and others in a new way
    D. increasing the participants' powers of logic and reasoning

15.____

16. In conducting a disciplinary interview, a supervisor finds that he must ask some highly personal questions which are relevant to the problem at hand.
    The interviewer is MOST likely to get truthful answers to these questions if he asks them
    A. early in the interview, before the interviewee has had a chance to become emotional
    B. in a manner so that the interviewee can answer them with a simple *yes* or *no*
    C. well into the interview, after rapport and trust have been established
    D. just after the close of the interview, so that the questions appear to be off the record

16.____

17. Suppose that, as a newly assigned manager, you observe that a supervisor in your division uses autocratic methods which are causing resentment among his subordinates.
    Of the following, the MOST likely reason for this supervisor's using such methods is that he
    A. was probably exposed to this type of supervision himself
    B. does not have an intuitive sense of tact, diplomacy, and consideration and no amount of training can change this
    C. received approval for use of such method from his former subordinates
    D. does not understand the basic concept of rewards and punishment in the practice of supervision

17.____

18. A newly appointed employee, Mr. Jones, was added to the staff of a supervisor who, because of the pressure of other work, turned him over to an experienced subordinate by saying, *Show Mr. Jones around and give him something to do.*
    On the basis of this experience, Mr. Jones' FIRST impression of his new position was most likely to have been
    A. *negative*, mainly because it appeared that his job was not worth his supervisor's attention
    B. *negative*, mainly because the more experienced subordinate would tend to emphasize the unpleasant aspects of the work
    C. *positive*, mainly because his supervisor wasted no time in assigning him to a subordinate
    D. *positive*, mainly because he saw himself working for a dynamic supervisor who expected immediate results

18.____

19. An employee who stays in one assignment for a number of years often develops a feeling of possessiveness concerning his knowledge of the job which may develop into a problem.
 Of the following, the BEST way for a supervisor to remedy this difficulty is to
 A. give the employee less important work to do
 B. point out minor errors as often as possible
 C. raise performance standards for all employees
 D. rotate the employee to a different assignment

20. A supervisor who tends to be supportive of his subordinates, in contrast to a supervisor who relies upon an authoritarian style of leadership, is more likely, in dealing with his staff, to have to listen to complaints, to have to tolerate emotionally upset employees, and even have to hear unreasonable and insulting remarks.
 Compared to the authoritarian supervisor, he is MORE likely to
 A. be unconsciously fearful of failure
 B. have an overriding interest in production
 C. have subordinates who are better educated
 D. receive accurate feedback information

KEY (CORRECT ANSWERS)

1.	B	11.	B
2.	B	12.	B
3.	B	13.	C
4.	A	14.	D
5.	B	15.	C
6.	C	16.	C
7.	B	17.	A
8.	C	18.	A
9.	C	19.	D
10.	C	20.	D

# TEST 2

DIRECTIONS: Each question or incomplete statement is followed by several suggested answers or completions. Select the one that BEST answers the question or completes the statement. *PRINT THE LETTER OF THE CORRECT ANSWER IN THE SPACE AT THE RIGHT.*

1. Assume that one of your subordinates, a supervisor in charge of a small unit in your bureau, asks your advice in handling a situation which has just occurred in his unit. On returning from a meeting, the supervisor notices that Jane Jones, the unit secretary, is not at her regular work location. Another employee had become faint, and the secretary accompanied this employee outdoors for some fresh air. It is a long-standing rule that no employee is permitted to leave the building during office hours except on official business or with the unit head's approval. Quite recently another employee was reprimanded by the supervisor for going out at 10 A.M. for a cup of coffee.
   Of the following, it would be BEST for you to advise the supervisor to
   A. circulate a memo within the unit, restating the department's regulation concerning leaving the building during office hours
   B. overlook this rule violation in view of the extenuating circumstances
   C. personally reprimand the unit secretary since all employees must be treated in the same way when official rules are broken
   D. tell the unit secretary that you should reprimand her, but that you've decided to overlook the rule infraction this time

1.____

2. Of the following, the MOST valid reason why the application of behavioral modification techniques to management of large organizations is not yet widely accepted by managers is these techniques are
   A. based mainly on research conducted under highly controlled conditions
   B. more readily adaptable to training unskilled employees
   C. incompatible with the validated *management-by-objectives* approach
   D. manipulative and incompatible with the democratic approach

2.____

3. Because of intensive pressures which have developed since the onset of the city's financial problems, the members of a certain bureau have begun to file grievances about their working conditions. These protests are accumulating at a much greater rate than normal and faster than they can be disposed of under the current state of affairs. Concerned about the possible effect of these unresolved matters on the productivity of the bureau at such a critical time, the administrator in charge decides to take immediate action to improve staff relations.
   With this intention in mind, he should
   A. explain to the staff why their grievances cannot be handled at the present time; then inform them that there will be a moratorium on the filing of additional grievances until the current backlog has been eliminated
   B. assemble all grievants at a special meeting and assure them that their problems will be handled in due course, but the current pressures preclude the prompt settling of their grievances

3.____

33

C. assign the assistant directors of the bureau to immediately schedule and conduct hearings on the accumulated grievances until the backlog is eliminated
D. suggest that the grievants again confer with their supervisors about their problems, orally rather than in writing, with direct appeal to him for such cases as are not resolved in this manner

4. A supervisor is attending a staff meeting with other accounting supervisors during which the participants are to propose various possible methods of dealing with a complex operational problem.
The one of the following procedures which will MOST likely produce an acceptable proposal for solving this problem at this meeting is for the
   A. group to agree at the beginning of the meeting on the kinds of approaches to the problem that are most likely to succeed
   B. conference leader to set a firm time limit on the period during which the participants are to present whatever ideas come to mind
   C. group to discuss each proposal fully before the next proposal is made
   D. conference leader to urge every participant in the meeting to present at least one proposal

4.____

5. Which one of the following types of communication systems would foster an authoritarian atmosphere in a large agency?
A communication system which
   A. is restricted to organizational procedures and specific job instructions
   B. provides information to employees about the rationale for their jobs
   C. informs employees about their job performance
   D. provides information about the relationship of employees' work to the agency's goals

5.____

6. According to most management experts, the one of the following which would generally have SERIOUS shortcomings as a component of a performance evaluation program is
   A. rating the performance of each subordinate against the performance of other subordinates
   B. limiting the appraisal to an evaluation of current performance
   C. rating each subordinate in terms of clearly stated, measurable job goals
   D. interviewing the subordinate to discuss present job performance and ways of improvement

6.____

7. Which of the following is consistent with the management-by-objectives approach as used in a fiscal affairs division of a large city agency?
   A. Performance goals for the division are established by the administrator, who requires daily progress reports for each accounting unit.
   B. Each subordinate accountant participates in setting his own short-term performance goals.
   C. A detailed set of short-term performance goals for each accountant is prepared by his supervisor.
   D. Objectives are established and progress evaluated by a committee of administrative accountants.

7.____

Questions 8-11.

DIRECTIONS: Questions 8 through 11 are to be answered on the basis of the following information.

Assume that you are the director of a small bureau, organized into three divisions. The bureau has a total of twenty employees: fourteen in professional titles and six in clerical titles. Each division has a chief who reports directly to you and who supervises five employees.

For Questions 8 through 11, you are to select the MOST appropriate training method, from the four choices given, based on the situation in the question:
- A. Lecture, with a small blackboard available
- B. Lecture, with audio-visual aids
- C. Conference
- D. Buddy system (experienced worker is accompanied by worker to be trained)

8. A major reorganization of your department was completed. You have decided to conduct a training session of about one hour's duration for all your subordinates in order to acquaint them with the new departmental structure as well as the new responsibilities which have been assigned to the divisions of your bureau.

9. Three assistant supervisors, each with one year of service in your department, are transferred to your bureau as part of the process of strengthening the major activity of your bureau. In connection with their duties, if they are required to do field visits to business firms located in the various industrial areas of the city.

10. The work of your bureau requires that various forms be processed sequentially through each of three divisions. In recent weeks, you have received complaints from the division chiefs that their production is being impeded by a lack of cooperation from the chiefs and workers in the other divisions.

11. In order to improve the efficiency of the department, your department head has directed that all bureaus hold weekly, thirty-minute-long training sessions for all employees, to review relevant work procedures.

12. Which one of the following actions is usually MOST appropriate for a manager to take in order to encourage and develop coordination of effort among different units or individuals within an organization?
    - A. Providing rewards to the most productive employees
    - B. Giving employees greater responsibility and the authority to exercise it
    - C. Emphasizing to the employees that it is important to coordinate their efforts
    - D. Explaining the goals of the organization to the employees and how their jobs relate to those goals

13. The management of time is one of the critical aspects of any supervisor's performance.
    Therefore, in evaluating a subordinate from the viewpoint of how he manages time, a supervisor should rate HIGHEST the subordinate who
    A. concentrates on each task as he undertakes it
    B. performs at a standard and predictable pace under all circumstances
    C. takes shortened lunch periods when he is busy
    D. tries to do two things simultaneously

14. A MAJOR research finding regarding employee absenteeism is that
    A. absenteeism is likely to be higher on hot days
    B. male employees tend to be absent more than female employees
    C. the way an employee is treated as a definite bearing on absenteeism
    D. the distance employees have to travel is one of the most important factors in absenteeism

15. Of the following, the supervisory behavior that is of GREATEST benefit to the organization is exhibited by supervisors who
    A. are strict with subordinates about following rules and regulations
    B. encourage subordinates to be interested in the work
    C. are willing to assist with subordinates' work on most occasions
    D. get the most done with available staff and resources

16. In order to maintain a proper relationship with a worker who is assigned to staff rather than line functions, a line supervisor should
    A. accept all recommendations of the staff worker
    B. include the staff worker in the conferences called by the supervisor for his subordinates
    C. keep the staff worker informed of developments in the area of his staff assignment
    D. require that the staff worker's recommendations be communicated to the supervisor through the supervisor's own superior

17. Of the following, the GREATEST disadvantage of placing a worker in a staff position under the direct supervision of the supervisor whom he advises is the possibility that the
    A. staff worker will tend to be insubordinate because of a feeling of superiority over the supervisor
    B. staff worker will tend to give advice of the type which the supervisor wants to hear or finds acceptable
    C. supervisor will tend to be mistrustful of the advice of a worker of subordinate rank
    D. supervisor will tend to derive little benefit from the advice because to supervise properly he should know at least as much as his subordinate

18. One factor which might be given consideration in deciding upon the optimum span of control of a supervisor over his immediate subordinates is the position of the supervisor in the hierarchy of the organization.
    It is generally considered proper that the number of subordinates immediately supervised by a higher, upper echelon, supervisor
    A. is unrelated to and tends to form no pattern with the number of supervised by lower level supervisors
    B. should be about the same as the number supervised by a lower level supervisor
    C. should be larger than the number supervised by a lower level supervisor
    D. should be smaller than the number supervised by a lower level supervisor

    18.____

19. Assume that you are a supervisor and have been assigned to assist the head of a large agency unit. He asks you to prepare a simple, functional organization chart of the unit.
    Such a chart would be USEFUL for
    A. favorably impressing members of the public with the important nature of the agency's work
    B. graphically presenting staff relationships which may indicate previously unknown duplications, overlaps, and gaps in job duties
    C. motivating all employees toward better performance because they will have a better understanding of job procedures
    D. subtly and inoffensively making known to the staff in the unit that you are now in a position of responsibility

    19.____

20. In some large organizations, management's traditional means of learning about employee dissatisfaction has been in the *open door policy*.
    This policy USUALLY means that
    A. management lets it be known that a management representative is generally available to discuss employees' questions, suggestions, and complaints
    B. management sets up an informal employee organization to establish a democratic procedure for orderly representation of employees
    C. employees are encouraged to attempt to resolve dissatisfactions at the lowest possible level of authority
    D. employees are provided with an address or box so that they may safely and anonymously register complaints

    20.____

KEY (CORRECT ANSWERS)

1.	B	11.	A
2.	A	12.	D
3.	D	13.	A
4.	B	14.	C
5.	A	15.	D
6.	A	16.	C
7.	B	17.	B
8.	B	18.	D
9.	D	19.	B
10.	C	20.	A

EXAMINATION SECTION
TEST 1

DIRECTIONS: Each question or incomplete statement is followed by several suggested answers or completions. Select the one that BEST answers the question or completes the statement. *PRINT THE LETTER OF THE CORRECT ANSWER IN THE SPACE AT THE RIGHT.*

1. The new head of a central filing unit, after studying a procedure in use, decided that it was unsatisfactory. He thereupon drew up an entirely new procedure which made no use of and ignored the existing procedure.
   This plan of action is, in general,
   A. *satisfactory*; a new broom sweeps clean
   B. *unsatisfactory*; any plan should use available resources to the utmost before resorting to new creation
   C. *satisfactory*; in general, use of part of an old procedure and part of a new procedure results sin an unworkable patchwork arrangement
   D. *unsatisfactory*; before deciding that the existing procedure was unusable, he should have requested that an independent, unbiased agency study the problem
   E. *satisfactory*; it is usually less time consuming to construct a new plan than to remedy an old one

1.____

2. Assume that you have broken a complex job into simpler and smaller components.
   After you have assigned a component to each employee, should you proceed to teach each employee a number of alternative methods for doing his job?
   A. *yes*; the more methods for performing a job an employee knows, the more chance there is that he will choose the one best suited to his abilities
   B. *No*; experienced employees should be permitted to decide how to perform the jobs assigned to them
   C. *Yes*; if several different methods are available, a desirable flexibility of operation results
   D. *No*; a single method for each job should be decided upon and taught
   E. *Yes*; the employees will have greater interest in their jobs

2.____

3. Assume that you are the head of a major staff unit and that a line unit has requested from your unit a special report to be completed in one day. After reviewing the request, you decide that much tie would be saved if two items which you know are superfluous are omitted from the report. You discuss the matter with the head of the other unit and he still insists that the two items are essential for his purposes.
   The one of the following actions which you should take at this stage is to
   A. plan to complete the report, including the two items, as expeditiously as possible
   B. write a memorandum to the department head giving both opinions fairly and asking for a decision

3.____

C. plan to complete the report without the two items, as expeditiously as possible
D. devise a plan for preparing the report without the two items which will permit you to add them later if they prove necessary although some time may be lost
E. again review the report with the line unit showing them why the two items are unnecessary

4. The one of the following functions of a supervisor which can be MOST successfully delegated is
   A. responsibility for accomplishing the unit's mission
   B. handling discipline
   C. checking completed work
   D. reporting to the bureau chief
   E. placing subordinates in the proper job

5. It is a standard operating procedure in an office which receives several thousand forms each week to have the file on clerk accumulate a week's receipts before filing them. The forms will not be examined for a period of one month after receipt.
   In comparison with daily filing, this procedure is, in general,
   A. *less satisfactory*; it keeps the files unnecessarily incomplete
   B. *more satisfactory*; it tends to reduce filing time
   C. *less satisfactory*; all information should be placed in a safe storage place as soon as possible
   D. *more satisfactory*; it tends to eliminate the prefiling period
   E. *less satisfactory*; it tends to build up an unnecessary period

6. Some organizations attempt to keep a constant backlog of work.
   This procedure is usually
   A. *undesirable*; reports are not ready when they are needed
   B. *desirable*; it tends to insure continuity of work flow
   C. *undesirable*; production records are too difficult to keep
   D. *desirable*; it tends to keep the employees under constant pressure
   E. *undesirable*; it tends to keep the employees under constant pressure

7. The first few times a procedure is carried through, a close check should be kept of all work times.
   The PRIMARY reason for this is to
   A. be able to present a clear picture of the situation
   B. determine if the employees understand the procedure
   C. evaluate the efficiency which may have been presented by the new procedure
   D. determine the efficiency of the employees
   E. permit revision of schedules

8. The one of the following pieces of information which is of LEAST importance in setting up the schedule for a given job is the time
   A. which is required to perform each component of the job
   B. when the source material will be available
   C. the job will take under adverse conditions
   D. by which the job must be completed
   E. employees will be available

9. Every employee should have a thorough knowledge of the organization of which he is a part.
   Of the following, the BEST justification for the above opinion is that
   A. the feeling of being a member of a team develops a responsible attitude toward one's everyday duties
   B. in an emergency, an employee may be called upon to perform duties other than his own
   C. the intricate details of an organization as complicated as a city department cannot easily be reduced to an organization chart
   D. an understanding of the different specialized units in an organization is often necessary to achieve the organization's given objective
   E. many city jobs are technical; thus, each employee should be trained to have more than a single narrow skill

10. The one of the following which is NOT a good rule in administering discipline is for you as a supervisor to
    A. reprimand the employee in private even though the fault was committed before others
    B. allow the employee a chance to reply to your criticism if he wishes
    C. be as specific as possible in criticizing the employee for his faults
    D. be sure you have all the facts before you reprimand an employee for an error he has committed
    E. allow an extended period to elapse after an error has been committed before reprimanding an employee

11. After you have submitted your annual evaluations of the work of your subordinates, one of them whose work has not been satisfactory complains to you that your evaluation was unjustified.
    For you to avoid discussing the evaluation but to point out two or three specific instances where the employee's work was below standard is
    A. *desirable*; an employee should be told what aspects of his work are unsatisfactory
    B. *undesirable*; once the evaluation has been submitted, there is no point in reconsidering it
    C. *desirable*; once the evaluation has been submitted, there is no point in reconsidering it but a discussion of the employee's weaknesses may help
    D. *undesirable*; it would have been better to explain how you arrived at your evaluation
    E. *desirable*; entering into a general argument is bad for the discipline of an organization

12. The chief of a central files bureau which has 50 employees customarily spends a considerable portion of his time in spot-checking the files, reviewing material being transferred from active to inactive files and similar activities.
    From the viewpoint of the department top management, the MOST pertinent evaluation which can be made on the basis of this information is that the
    A. supervisor is conscientious and hardworking
    B. bureau may need additional staff
    C. supervisor has not made a sufficient delegation of authority and responsibility
    D. bureau needs an in-service training course as the work of its employees requires an abnormal amount of review
    E. filing system employed may be inadequate

    12.____

13. Assume that you are in charge of a unit with 40 employees. The department head requests immediate preparation of a special and rather complicated report which will take about a day to complete if everyone in your unit works on it.
    After breaking the job into simple components and assigning each component to an employee, should more than one person be instructed on the procedure to be followed on each component?
    A. *No*; the procedure would be a waste of time in this instance
    B. *Yes*; it is always desirable to have a replacement available in the event of illness or any other emergency
    C. *No*; in general, as long as an employee's job performance is satisfactory, there is no need to train an alternate
    D. *Yes*; the presence of more than one person in a unit who can perform a given task tends to prevent the formation of a bottleneck
    E. *No*; there is, in general, no need to train more than one employee in the performance of a special job

    13.____

14. A new employee who has shown that she is capable of performing superior work during the first month of her employment falls far below this standard after the first month.
    For the supervisor to wait until the end of the probationary period and then recommend that she be discharged if her work is still unsatisfactory is
    A. *undesirable*; she should have been discharged when her work became unsatisfactory
    B. *desirable*; there is no place in the civil service for unsatisfactory employees
    C. *undesirable*; he should immediately attempt to determine the cause of the poor performance
    D. *desirable*; the employee is entitled to an opportunity to prove herself
    E. *undesirable*; the employee is obviously capable of performing good work and simply requires some guidance from the supervisor

    14.____

15. In order to make sure that work is completed on time, the unit supervisor should   15.____
    A. use the linear method of delegating responsibility
    B. pitch in and do as much of the work himself as he can
    C. schedule the work and keep himself informed of its progress
    D. not assign more than one person to any one task
    E. know the capabilities of his subordinates

16. One of the more effective ways to obtain optimum performance from employees   16.____
    is to keep them off balance by not letting them feel secure in the job; to permit
    an employee to feel secure is to invite him to settle into a comfortable rut.
    The point of view expressed in this statement is
    A. *correct*; studies have shown that the degree of effort put forth on a job
       generally varies directly with the degree of job insecurity
    B. *incorrect*; studies have shown that a relatively high degree of security is
       conducive to best job performance
    C. *correct*; while studies have shown that there is little relationship between
       security and job performance, what tendencies are present to support the
       point of view expressed
    D. *incorrect*; studies have shown that there is little relationship between
       security and job performance and what tendencies are present are
       opposed to the point of view expressed
    E. *correct*; while no specific studies have been made in this field, analogous
       studies made in similar fields show that permitting a feeling of security to
       develop results in decreased job performance

Questions 17-19.

DIRECTIONS: Questions 17 through 19 are to be answered on the basis of the following
              paragraph.

The supervisor of a large clerical and statistical division has assigned to one of the units
under his supervision the preparation of a special statistical report required by the department
head. The unit accepted the assignment without comment but soon ran into considerable
difficulty because no one in his unit had had any statistical training.

17. If a result of this lack of training is that the report is not completed on time,   17.____
    although everyone has done all that could be expected, the responsibility for
    the failure rests with
    A. the department head   B. the supervisor
    C. the unit head   D. the employees in the unit
    E. no one

18. This incident indicates that the supervisory staff has insufficient knowledge of   18.____
    employee
    A. capabilities
    B. reaction to increased demands
    C. on-the-job training needs
    D. work habits
    E. ability to perform ordinary assignments

19. After working on the report for two days, the unit head notifies the supervisor 19._____
that he will not be able to get the report out in the required time. He states that
his staff will be completely trained in another day or two and that after
preparing the report will be a simple matter. At this stage, the supervisor
decides to have the statistical unit prepare the report.
This action on the part of the supervisor is
   A. *undesirable*; the unit head should be given an incentive to continue with
      his training program which may produce good results
   B. *desirable*; it is the most effective way in which the supervisor can show
      his displeasure with the unit head's failure
   C. *undesirable*; it may adversely affect the morale of the unit
   D. *desirable*; it will generally result in a better report completed in a shorter
      time
   E. *undesirable*; the time spent training the unit will be completely wasted

20. A supervisor criticizes a subordinate's work by telling him that he is disappointed 20._____
with it. The supervisor states that the work is completely unsatisfactory, shows
where it is bad, and says that improvement is expected.
This approach is usually
   A. *good*; the employee knows just where he stands
   B. *poor*; some favorable comment should be made at the same time if
      possible
   C. *good*; it is good policy to keep this type of interview as short as possible
   D. *poor*; the employee should be asked to explain why his work is poor
   E. *good*; the supervisor did not criticize the subordinate in front of other
      employees

Questions 21-25.

DIRECTIONS: Column I below lists five kinds of statistical data which are to be transformed
into a chart or a graph for incorporation into the department annual report.
Column II lists nine different kinds of graphs or charts. For each type of
information listed in Column I, select the chart or graph from Column II by
means of which it should be demonstrated.

<u>COLUMN I</u>   <u>COLUMN II</u>

21. The relationship between employees' 21._____
occupational classification and their salaries,
for all employees by occupational classification,
showing minimum, maximum, and average
salary in each group.

22. A comparison of the number of employees in the 22._____
department, the departmental budget the number
of employees in the operating divisions and the
operating division budget for each year over a
ten-year period.

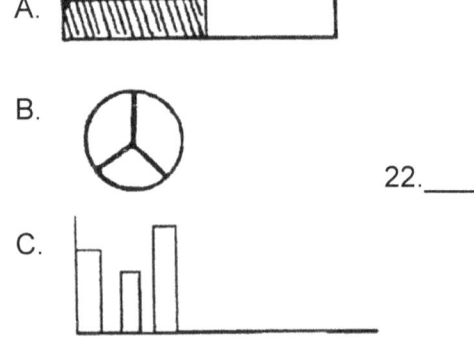

COLUMN I	COLUMN II
23. The amount of money spent for each of the department's 10 most important functions during the past year.	D.  23.____
24. The percentage of the department's budget spent for each of the department's activities for each year over a ten-year period.	E.  24.____
25. The number of each kind of employee employed in the department over a period of twenty years and the total number of employees in the department for each of these periods.	F.  25.____
	G. 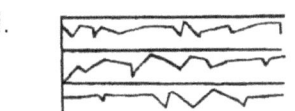
	H.
	I.

KEY (CORRECT ANSWERS)

1. B
2. D
3. A
4. C
5. B

6. B
7. E
8. C
9. A
10. E

11. D
12. C
13. A
14. C
15. C

16. B
17. B
18. A
19. D
20. B

21. F
22. D
23. C
24. H
25. G

TEST 2

DIRECTIONS: Each question or incomplete statement is followed by several suggested answers or completions. Select the one that BEST answers the question or completes the statement. *PRINT THE LETTER OF THE CORRECT ANSWER IN THE SPACE AT THE RIGHT.*

1. The report of the head of Unit Y to his bureau chief on the performance of a new clerical employee indicates that the performance is not up to the expected standard. After reading the report, the bureau chief transferred the employee to Unit X.
   This action on the part of the bureau chief was
   A. in line with good personal practice; an employee who does poorly in one place may do better in another
   B. premature; an attempt to discover the cause of the poor performance should be made first
   C. desirable; personnel reports become meaningless unless acted upon at once
   D. undesirable; unsatisfactory employees should be dismissed and not transferred from unit to unit
   E. in the best interest of the organization; whenever a supervisor cannot get along with a subordinate for whatever reason, it is desirable to transfer the subordinate

   1.____

2. Suppose that you have been consulted by a department head who wishes to initiate an in-service training course in his department. The department head suggests that, as a first step, a training course be initiated for supervisors in the department.
   This suggestion is BEST characterized as
   A. *undesirable*; the supervisors are generally the persons least in need of work incentives
   B. *desirable*; it is generally cheaper and more effective to train a few supervisors than a large number of employees
   C. *undesirable*; supervisors may be held up to ridicule if they are isolated for training
   D. *desirable*; trained supervisors are needed to train employees
   E. *undesirable*; employees should be trained before supervisors

   2.____

3. Any person thoroughly familiar with the specific steps in a particular class of work is well qualified to serve as a training course instructor in that work.
   This statement is erroneous CHIEFLY because
   A. it is practically impossible for any instructor to be acquainted with all the specific steps sin a particular class of work
   B. what is true of one class of work is not necessarily true of other types of work
   C. a qualified instructor cannot be expected to have detailed information about many specific fields

   3.____

D. the steps in any type of work are usually interrelated and not independent or unique
E. the quantity of information possessed by an instructor does not bear a direct relationship to the quality of instruction

4. Of the following, the MOST significant argument against making it compulsory for civil service employees to attend a training course is that
   A. unwilling trainees will be penalized in any event by non-promotion
   B. most training requires additional time and expense on the part of the trainee
   C. training is highly desirable but not absolutely essential for adequate job performance
   D. incompetent work is generally reflected in poor service ratings
   E. trainees must be receptive if training is to be successful

4.____

5. There are four basic systems of job evaluation which have been extensively used by government and industry.
   The one of the following which is NOT one of these is the _____ system.
   A. Benchmark   B. Factor Comparison
   C. Point   D. Job Classification
   E. Ranking

5.____

6. Of the following, the CHIEF advantage derived by filling all vacancies in an organization by promotion from below rather than from outside the organization is that such a procedure
   A. fills existing vacancies from the widest possible recruitment base
   B. stimulates individual employees to improve their work habits
   C. avoids personality difficulties likely to arise when an employee is assigned to supervise former colleagues
   D. indirectly coordinates the work of different units by interchange of personnel
   E. encourages reorientation and review of administrative procedures

6.____

7. Of the following, the CHIEF justification for a periodic classification audit is that
   A. salaries should be readjusted at frequent intervals
   B. some degree of personnel turnover should always be expected
   C. a career service requires regular promotion opportunities
   D. employees require frequent stimulation and encouragement
   E. positions frequently change over a period of time

7.____

8. A classification analyst sorts jobs horizontally and vertically.
   Of the following, the LEAST important job factor to be considered with respect to vertical placement is
   A. independence of action and decision
   B. consequence of errors
   C. kind and character of work performed
   D. degree of supervision received
   E. determination of policy

8.____

9. Assume that you have been assigned to prepare a plan for conducting a large scale job classification survey.
Of the following, the BEST suggestion for reducing the number of appeals from the final allocations likely to be received after the classification study has been completed is to
   A. have supervisors check statements of employees on classification questionnaires
   B. allocate present positions to proposed classes according to jurisdictional assignments
   C. adjust salary to present level of work performed by employees
   D. allow employee participation throughout the classification process
   E. postpone controversial problems until simpler problems have been solved and a general blueprint laid down

9._____

10. A comment made by an employee about a training course was, *Oh, I suppose it's important for the job but it's a waste of time for me just to sit in that course and yawn while the instructor rambles on."*
The fundamental error in training methodology to which this criticism points is failure to provide
    A. goals for the students
    B. for individual differences
    C. connecting links between new and old material
    D. for student participation
    E. motivation for the subject matter of the course

10._____

11. You are preparing a long report addressed to your superior on a study which you have conducted for him.
The one of the following sections which should come FIRST in the report is a
    A. description of the working procedure utilized in the study
    B. description of the situation which exists
    C. summary of the conclusions of the survey
    D. discussion of possible objections to the report and their refutation
    E. description of the method of installing the recommendations

11._____

12. While setting up a reporting system to help the department planning section, an administrator proposed the policy that no overlap or duplication be permitted even if it meant that some minor areas were left uncovered.
This policy is
    A. *undesirable*; overlap is frequently necessary
    B. *desirable*; the presence of overlap and duplication indicates defective planning
    C. *undesirable*; setting up general policy in advance of the specific reporting system may lead to inflexibility
    D. *desirable*; it is not necessary to get complete coverage in order to be able to plan operations
    E. *undesirable*; duplication is preferable to leaving any area uncovered

12._____

4 (#2)

Questions 13-15.

DIRECTIONS: Questions 13 through 15 are to be answered on the basis of the following paragraph.

Prior to revising its child care program, a department feels that it is necessary to get some information from the mothers served by the existing program in order to determine where changes are required. A questionnaire is to be constructed to obtain this information.

13. Of the following points which can be taken into consideration in the construction of the questionnaire, the one which is of LEAST importance is
    A. that the data are to be put into punch cards
    B. the aspects of the program which seem to be in need of change
    C. the type of person who will fill out the questionnaire
    D. testing the questionnaire for ambiguity in advance of general distribution
    E. setting up a control group so that answers received can be compared to a standard

13.____

14. To discuss this questionnaire with all mothers who have been asked to answer it, before they actually fill it out, is
    A. *desirable*; the mothers may be able to offer valuable suggestions for changes in the form of the questionnaire
    B. *undesirable*; it is of some value but consumes too much valuable time
    C. *desirable*; cooperation and uniform interpretation will tend to be achieved
    D. *undesirable*; it may cause the answers to be biased
    E. *desirable*; the group will tend to support the program

14.____

15. Of the following items included in the questionnaire, the one which will be of LEAST assistance for comparing attitudes toward the program among different kinds of persons is
    A. name
    B. address
    C. age
    D. place of birth
    E. education

15.____

16. You have been asked, to prepare for public distribution, a statement dealing with a controversial matter.
    Of the following approaches, the one which would usually be MOST effective is to present your department's point of view
    A. as tersely as possible with no reference to any other matters
    B. developed from ideas and facts well known to most readers
    C. and show all the statistical data and techniques which were used in arriving at it
    D. in such a way that the controversial parts are omitted
    E. substantiated by supporting quotations from persons in the specialized field even if they are not well known

16.____

50

5 (#2)

17. During a conference of administrative staff personnel, the department head discussing the letter prepared for his signature stated, *"Use no more words than are necessary to express your meaning."*
Following this rule in letter writing is, in general,
    A. *desirable*; considerable time will be saved in the preparation of correspondence
    B. *undesirable*; it is frequently necessary to elaborate on an explanation in order to make certain that the reader will understand
    C. *desirable*; terse statements give government letters a business-like air which impresses readers favorably
    D. *undesirable*; terse statements are generally cold and formal and produce an unfavorable reaction in the reader
    E. *desirable*; the use of more words than are necessary is likely to obscure the meaning and tire the reader

17.____

18. While you are designing the layout for a departmental procedure manual, it is suggested that you carefully arrange your reading material so that there will be a minimum amount of blank space on the page.
Of the following judgments of this suggestion, the one which is the MOST valid basis for action is that it is
    A. *bad*; readability and ease of reference will be decreased
    B. *good*; the cost of production can be decreased considerably without any great disadvantage
    C. *of little or no importance*; more or less blank space on the page will not affect the value of the manual
    D. *good*; it will make for a smaller, easier to handle book
    E. *bad*; replacement of outdated pages is made more difficult by having more material on a page

18.____

19. After the planning of an employee's procedure manual had been completed, the suggestion was made that the manual should be prepared and arranged so that changes could be made readily.
Of the following decisions with respect to this suggestion, the one which is MOST desirable from the viewpoint of good administration is that the suggestions should
    A. not be considered as it is generally impossible to prepare a satisfactory manual which will take everything into consideration
    B. be followed only if it does not conflict with the planned layout
    C. be used even if it is somewhat more costly than the planned layout
    D. be noted and acted upon at the next revision of the manual
    E. not be considered as this type of manual is more difficult to maintain properly

19.____

20. Assume that you are in charge of preparing a procedure manual of about 100 pages for a large clerical unit. After you have decided to use a looseleaf format, one of your subordinates proposes that only one side of the page be printed.

20.____

51

This proposal is
- A. *good*; replacement of obsolete pages is made easier
- B. *poor*; cost is increased
- C. *good*; provision is automatically made for employee's notes
- D. *poor*; it will increase the size of the manual, making it more difficult to use
- E *good*; indexing will be made easier

21. It may be assumed that if all departments had qualified personnel officers, not all departments would be lacking adequate training programs. However, the most cursory examination of the situation will show that some departments do not have adequate training programs. Thus, we must conclude that some of them lack qualified personnel officers.
The argument presented in the report is
- A. *correct*; the conclusion follows logically from the assumption and the facts
- B. *not correct*; what can be concluded is that no department has a qualified personnel officer
- C. *not correct*; no conclusion with respect to the presence of personnel officers in departments can be drawn from the information
- D. *not correct*; what can be concluded is that the absence of an adequate training program in a department implies the absence of a personnel officer
- E. *correct*; but the conclusion is false as the hypothesis is not true

21.____

22. In a study of the relationship between a fixed discipline policy and the incidence of lateness, it would be MOST informative to have data proving the statement:
- A. In those organizations in which there are no fixed discipline policy, the incidence of lateness is variable.
- B. The incidence of lateness has not decreased in those organizations where fixed discipline policies have been abandoned.
- C. The incidence of lateness and the discipline policy vary from organization to organization.
- D. Discipline policies sometimes ignore the problem of lateness.
- E. In organizations with a fixed discipline policy, the incidence of lateness is variable.

22.____

23. The data prove that an increase in the number of clerks performing filing work results in an increased cost per item filed.
On the basis of these data, we can be certain that
- A. if filing costs per item filed increase, it is caused by an increase in the number of clerks filing
- B. if filing costs per item filed decrease, the number of clerks filing cannot be increasing
- C. if the number of clerks filing is changed, the unit cost per filing will change
- D. if the number of clerks filing is not increased, the cost per unit filed will not increase
- E. if the number of clerks filing is decreased, the cost per item filed will decrease

23.____

24. Each unit either has sufficient space assigned to it or it has not. No unit which has insufficient space assigned to it has neglected to ask for additional space. From these data, we can state
   A. units with sufficient space have not asked for additional space
   B. only units which have sufficient space have not asked for additional space
   C. nothing about the relationship between the need for additional space and requests made for additional space
   D. all units which have requested additional space have insufficient space
   E. no units which have requested additional space have sufficient space

24.____

25. One argument which is presented against a strict career system in the civil service is as follows:
The employees who are recruited today for low-level jobs become the administrators of tomorrow. At the present time the employees we are attracting for the low-level jobs are untrained and poorly educated. Thus, it follows that the administrators of tomorrow will be untrained and poorly educated.
The one of the following which is a CORRECT criticism of the reasoning is that
   A. the argument is logically correct but the conclusion is false as the hypothesis that we are attracting untrained and poorly educated people for our low-level job is false
   B. the conclusion does not follow logically from hypotheses
   C. the argument is logically correct, but the conclusion is false because it is a false hypothesis that tomorrow's administrators will come from employees who hold low-level jobs
   D. the argument is logically correct and the conclusion is correct
   E. while the argument is logically correct and the hypotheses are not demonstrably false, the argument ignores the realities of the case that those who are untrained today may be trained tomorrow

25.____

KEY (CORRECT ANSWERS)

1.	B	11.	C
2.	D	12.	E
3.	E	13.	E
4.	E	14.	C
5.	A	15.	A
6.	B	16.	B
7.	E	17.	E
8.	C	18.	A
9.	D	19.	C
10.	D	20.	A

21. C
22. B
23. B
24. B
25. B

TEST 3

DIRECTIONS: Each question or incomplete statement is followed by several suggested answers or completions. Select the one that BEST answers the question or completes the statement. *PRINT THE LETTER OF THE CORRECT ANSWER IN THE SPACE AT THE RIGHT.*

1. Surveying modern administration, it becomes clear that there is GREATEST need at present for administrators with
   A. a good knowledge of personnel administration
   B. the ability to write good reports
   C. a working knowledge of modern methods analysis
   D. a broad rather than specialized viewpoint
   E. the ability to analyze complicated fiscal programs

2. The one of the following which is a fundamental obstacle to effective planning in MOST governmental agencies is
   A. inadequate staff or resources
   B. the absence of the properly centralized administration
   C. the absence of clearly defined objective and constituent programs
   D. the neglect of analysis of ways and means
   E. the absence of functional boundaries for units and individuals

3. A department consists of several independent bureaus, each responsible to the commissioner for its own planning, operation, and reporting, a central personnel unit and the commissioner's office consisting of a secretary and several clerks to handle public relations.
   The one of the following *undesirable* characteristics which is MOST likely to arise in this organization is
   A. absence of planning
   B. weak and ineffectual leadership
   C. failure to have employees properly trained
   D. a lack of an easily understandable goal
   E. duplication of work

4. The one of the following practices which is MOST likely to lead to confusion, recrimination and jurisdictional conflict among the bureaus of a department is the failure to
   A. make clear and unambiguous assignments
   B. systematically subdivide the work
   C. explain general policy to those responsible for its achievement
   D. allocate equitably available resources
   E. set up uniform operating procedures for all units

5. The one of the following which is MOST likely to occur in an over-specialized administrative set-up is
   A. inability to recruit proper personnel to fill over-specialized positions
   B. improper supervision
   C. failure of employees to realize the broad implications of their work

D. lack of proper decentralization of authority, as emphasis on specialization goes hand-in-hand with over-centralization
E. inability to solve technical problems which are not entirely in one specialty

6. Of the following, the LEAST valid reason for a department head continuing to require that a weekly report be forwarded to him, is that the report forms a basis for
   A. measuring performance
   B. making decisions
   C. revising policy
   D. the execution of the mission of the unit which receives it
   E. the operation of the unit which is required to prepare it

7. Administrators must learn not to farm out essential functions to unintegrated agencies, but to organize all responsibilities in unified but decentralized hierarchies.
   A problem which an administrator may be expected to face if he has not learned this is that
   A. the organization fails to develop administrators capable of independent action
   B. issues will not be posed at the level where decisions should be made
   C. relationships with the public will not be satisfactory
   D. it will be difficult to achieve administrative control or get agreement on departmental action
   E. individual agencies will be unable to complete the work scheduled

8. The central staff planning unit within any organization includes in its functions helping to plan policy at one extreme and planning detailed execution at the other extreme.
   With respect to the actual execution, the planning activity should
   A. have no concern with it
   B. simply forward and explain new plans
   C. have only the responsibility of explaining in the form of plans the objectives of top management
   D. keep track of how the plans are working out but make no attempt to supervise their execution
   E. supervise the execution of new plans

9. The head of a department assigned final responsibility for the training function to the personnel office.
   This assignment was
   A. *undesirable*; this type of centralization prevents a staff organization from carrying out staff functions
   B. *desirable*; experience has shown that centralization of this type results in more efficient and economic operation
   C. *undesirable*; the personnel office usually does not have the technical "know how" to carry this responsibility
   D. *desirable*; if training is left to the line officials, it never is accomplished
   E. *undesirable*; this responsibility must rest with the supervisor

10. A department head insisted that operating officials participate in the development of new procedures along with the planning section.
    Participation of this type is, on the whole,
    A. *desirable*; operating realities are more likely to be considered
    B. *undesirable*; the inclusion of conflicting views before the plan is drawn may result in no plan
    C. *desirable*; plans will be more flexible and objectives more clearly defined
    D. *undesirable*; the operating officials should decide to what extent they wish to participate with no pressure from the top
    E. *desirable*; to back down on a procedure once it has been decided upon is a sign of weakness

11. Much of the current criticism of the administration of large organizations is basically a criticism of our failure to place the same emphasis on accountability that we do on authority and responsibility.
    The one of the following acts which is MOST likely to insure accountability for the discharge of responsibilities inherent in the delegation of authority is the
    A. establishment of appropriate reports and controls
    B. organization of a methods analysis section
    C. delegation of authority so made as to support functional or homogeneous activities
    D. delegation of authority so made as to preserve unity of command
    E. decentralization of responsibility and authority

12. This statement has been made:
    A man who is a top-notch executive in one organization would make a top-notch executive in any other organization, even if the organizations are as diverse as a sales agency and a research foundation.
    This statement is, in general,
    A. *correct*; the characteristics required for a good executive are invariant with respect to organization
    B. *incorrect*; there is no way of predicting how a good executive in one organization would be in any other
    C. *correct*; while the characteristics required for a good executive vary from organization to organization, the common core requirements are great enough to insure similar performance
    D. *incorrect*; although some prediction can be made, different types of organizations require different types of executives
    E. *correct*; success as an executive does not depend upon "characteristics" but on the man; if he is able to direct and execute in one organization he will be able to do so in any other

13. Reported information is not needed at levels higher than those at which decisions are made on the basis of the information reported.
    This statement is, in general,
    A. *correct*; if no action is to be taken on the basis of the information, the information is unnecessary
    B. *incorrect*; all information is of importance in arriving at a sound decision

C. *correct*; levels below the one at which the decision is made have need of the information
D. *incorrect*; levels below the one at which the decision is made do not have need of the information
E. *correct*; decisions should be made on the basis of information reported

14. Of the following, the characteristic of an organization which BEST shows that the organizational hierarchy is effective is that
    A. the department head commands the respect of the employees
    B. the organization is sufficiently flexible to assume functions in fields not related to his major field of endeavor
    C. responsibility has been appropriately delegated throughout the organization
    D. the department continues to function effectively even though there is continual turnover in the higher supervisory ranks
    E. no employee in the organization is subject to orders from more than one source

15. It is only because the primary purpose of traditional discipline has been to preserve the structure of command that a need has arisen for ameliorative safeguards such as a formal statement of "cause," right of hearing, and right of appeal.
    The BEST current practice with respect to discipline is that
    A. few ameliorative safeguards of the kind enumerated are desirable as their presence hurts the public service
    B. discipline is a means of controlling deviations from established authority
    C. the safeguards enumerated are not sufficient for the protection of the employee
    D. discipline should be based upon education, persuasion, and consultation
    E. unquestioned obedience to each order should not be expected but that a supervisor should be prepared at all times to demonstrate the reasonableness of his requests

16. Of the following types of work, the one for which a manual process is MOST usually to be preferred over a mechanized process is one in which the transactions are very
    A. numerous   B. similar   C. dissimilar
    D. predictable E. unpredictable

17. Work flow charts are used in an organization PRIMARILY because they
    A. indicate present and future objectives clearly
    B. are frequently used records
    C. clearly indicate when each operation will be performed
    D. summarize the work procedures of the organization
    E. tend to clarify thinking by presenting certain facts clearly

5 (#3)

18. With respect to a report prepared by an IBM installation, the one of the following changes which is LEAST likely to cause a change in the procedure for preparing the report is a change in the
    A. volume of work
    B. source documents
    C. final report
    D. employees assigned
    E. time allowed for the preparation of the report

    18._____

19. The one of the following which is NOT necessarily a characteristic of a good buying procedure is that it
    A. provides for proper analysis of purchases made
    B. is simple
    C. makes provision for substitutions where possible and necessary
    D. makes sealed bids mandatory
    E. recruits many bidders

    19._____

20. Data relating to the operation of any unit should be accumulated and periodically summarized and analyzed PRIMARILY in order to
    A. point out the most efficient and least efficient workers
    B. determine the relative value of each procedure
    C. locate the elements of an operation which are unusually efficient or inefficient
    D. evaluate the importance of maintaining operating records and quotas
    E. compare the work performed by comparable units

    20._____

21. Of the following, the MAJOR function of an administrative planning and research staff units is to
    A. investigate trouble points in the organization
    B. reorganize inefficient units
    C. assist the executive to plan future operations
    D. conduct continuous investigations and planning
    E. write the necessary operation and procedure manuals

    21._____

22. The one of the following which does NOT require definition when setting up a work measurement system is the
    A. level of work accomplishment at which to measure
    B. work unit in which to measure
    C. time unit by which to measure
    D. acceptable quota for each activity
    E. reporting system to be used

    22._____

23. During a discussion of the time unit that would be appropriate to measure employee-time in a work measurement program in a public agency, the man-day was suggested.
    This unit is
    A. *satisfactory*; record keeping will be kept to a minimum
    B. *unsatisfactory*; it will be difficult to verify the unit against official time records

    23._____

C. *satisfactory*; it will be easy to verify the unit against official time records
D. *unsatisfactory*; its use will unnecessarily complicate record keeping
E. *satisfactory*; it permits more meaningful comparisons to be made between equal periods of time

24. As part of a space layout survey, an administrator instructed his subordinates to study the flow of work and sequence of operating procedures.
His MAJOR purposes in doing this was to determine
    A. the physical distribution and movement of personnel, material, and equipment
    B. the amount of space which is available and the amount of space which will be required
    C. the order in which the component steps in the different procedures are performed
    D. what future requirements will be, based on observable present trend
    E. how the distribution of personnel to various organization units is related to their space requirements

24.____

25. Before discussing a proposed office layout, the administrative officer stated, *"We intend to have a minimum number of private offices. We will assign private offices only where quiet is deemed essential or confidential conferences are required."*
The one of the following which is usually the MOST valid reason for this rule is that it
    A. permits proper placing of employees who deal with the public
    B. makes it easier to locate supervisors near the units they control
    C. tends to ensure that the work of each unit will flow continually forward within itself
    D. allows placing complementary units close together
    E. makes clerical supervision easier

25.____

KEY (CORRECT ANSWERS)

1.	D		11.	A
2.	C		12.	D
3.	E		13.	A
4.	A		14.	C
5.	C		15.	D
6.	E		16.	C
7.	D		17.	E
8.	D		18.	D
9.	E		19.	D
10.	A		20.	C

21. D
22. D
23. D
24. A
25. E

EXAMINATION SECTION
TEST 1

DIRECTIONS: Each question or incomplete statement is followed by several suggested answers or completions. Select the one that BEST answers the question or completes the statement. *PRINT THE LETTER OF THE CORRECT ANSWER IN THE SPACE AT THE RIGHT.*

1. The number of subordinates that can be supervised directly by one person tends to
    A. *increase* as the level of supervision progresses from the first-line supervisory level to the management level
    B. *decrease* as the duties of the subordinates increase in difficulty and complexity
    C. *decrease* with an increase in the knowledge and experience of the subordinates
    D. *increase* as the physical distance between supervisor and subordinates, as well as between the individual subordinate, increases

1.____

2. A study of the supervision of employees in an agency reveals that the bureau chiefs are reluctant to delegate responsibility and authority to their assistants. This study is MOST likely to reveal, in addition, that
    A. the organizational structure of this agency should be centralized
    B. the bureau chiefs tend to spend too much of their time on minor aspects of their work
    C. the number of employees supervised by bureau chiefs is excessive
    D. significant deviations from planned performance are not called to the attention of the bureau chiefs

2.____

3. The delegation of responsibility and authority to subordinates by their superior generally does NOT
    A. facilitate a division of labor or the development of specialization
    B. permit the superior to carry out programs of work that exceed his immediate personal limits of physical energy and knowledge
    C. result in a downward transfer of work, both mental and manual
    D. involve a transfer of ultimate responsibility from superior to subordinate

3.____

4. Horizontal coordination is achieved when the various units of a bureau work with mutual harmony and assistance.
The achievement of such coordination is generally made MORE difficult when the chief of a large bureau
    A. conducts periodic conferences with supervisors of his operating units
    B. delegates some of his coordinating tasks to a staff assistant
    C. increases the number of specialized units in his bureau and the degree of their specialization
    D. transfers subordinates from one to another of his operating units to broaden their understanding of the bureau's work

4.____

5. Some subdivision of work is imperative in large-scale operations. However, in subdividing work, the superior should adopt the methods that have the greatest number of advantages and the fewest disadvantages.
The one of the following that is MOST likely to result from subdivision of work is
   A. measuring work performed by employees is made more difficult
   B. authority and responsibility for performance of particular operations are not clearly defined
   C. standardizing work processes is made more difficult
   D. work is delayed in passing between employees and between operating units

5.____

6. In developing a system for controlling the production of a bureau, the bureau chief should give consideration to reducing the fluctuations in the bureau's work load.
Of the following, the technique that is generally LEAST helpful in reducing fluctuations in work load is]
   A. staffing the bureau so that it can handle peak loads
   B. maintaining a controlled backlog of work
   C. regulating the order of steps in work processes
   D. changing the order of steps in work processes

6.____

7. The flow of work in an organization may be divided and channeled according to either a serial method or a parallel method. Under the serial method, the work moves through a single channel with each job progressing step by step through various work stations where a worker at each station completes a particular step of the job. Under the parallel method, the jobs are distributed among a number of workers, each worker completing all the steps of a job.
The MOST accurate of the following statements regarding these two methods of dividing the flow of work is that
   A. the training or break-in time necessary for workers to acquire processing skills is generally shorter under the parallel method
   B. the serial method enables the workers to obtain a fuller understanding of the significance of their work
   C. the parallel method tends to minimize the need for control devices to keep track of individual jobs in process
   D. flexibility in the use of available staff is generally increased under the serial method

7.____

8. The executive who has immediate responsibility for a group of functions should have the right to decide what the structure of his organization shall be.
In making such decision, the executive should realize that
   A. the lower the competence of a staff, the more important it is to maintain a sound organizational structure
   B. the productivity of a competent staff will not be affected by an impairment in organizational structure
   C. the productivity of a staff whose level of competency is low cannot be improved by an improvement in organizational structure
   D. where there is a sound organizational structure there must of necessity be a sound organization

8.____

9. Of the following means that a bureau chief may utilize in training his understudy, the LEAST acceptable one is for him to
   A. give the understudy assignments which other employees find too difficult or unpleasant
   B. discuss with the understudy the important problems that confront the bureau chief
   C. rotate the assignments given the understudy
   D. give the understudy an opportunity to attend some of the meetings of bureau chiefs

10. Of the following practices and techniques that may be employed by the conference leader, the one that the conference leader should ordinarily AVOID is
    A. permitting certain participants to leave the conference to get back to their work when the discussion has reached the point where their special interests or qualifications are no longer involved
    B. encouraging the participants to take full written notes for later comparison with the minutes of the meeting
    C. helping a participant extricate himself from an awkward position in which the participant has placed himself by an ill-advised remark
    D. translating the technical remarks of a speaker for the benefit of some participants who would otherwise fail to grasp the meaning of the remarks

11. In assigning work to his subordinates, a supervisor is MOST likely to lose the respect of his subordinate if he
    A. reviews with a new employee the main points of an oral order issued to this employee
    B. issues written orders instead of oral orders when a subordinate has repeatedly failed to carry out oral orders
    C. gives oral orders regarding a task which the subordinate has performed satisfactorily in the past
    D. gives an oral order which he feels the subordinate will not carry out

12. Both Agency X and Agency Y have district offices in all areas of the city. In Agency X, the activities of the various districts are administered under centralized control, whereas in Agency U the activities of the various district offices are administered under decentralized control.
    The one of the following which is MORE characteristic of Agency X than of Agency Y is that in Agency X
    A. activities of the district offices can more readily be adapted to meet the problems of the district served
    B. there are greater opportunities for district administration to develop resourcefulness
    C. agency policies can be carried out with greater uniformity
    D. decisions are made by individuals closer to the points at which problems arise

13. Of the following training methods, the one that is generally MOST valuable in teaching employees new clerical skills is
    A. organized group discussion
    B. individual instruction on the job
    C. use of visual aids, such as charts and pictures
    D. supervised reading, research, and inspection

14. Department X maintains offices in each district of the city. Data gathered by the district offices are submitted monthly to the main office on a standard set of forms which are somewhat complicated.
    Of the following methods of issuing detailed instructions for filling out the forms properly, the one generally considered MOST acceptable is
    A. incorporating the instructions in the department's procedure manual
    B. including an instruction sheet with each package of blank forms sent to a district office
    C. printing the instructions on the back of each form
    D. conducting periodic staff conferences devoted exclusively to discussions of the proper method of filling out the form

15. The one of the following which is usually LEAST affected by an increase in the personnel of an organization is the
    A. problems of employee relationships
    B. average amount of work performed by an employee
    C. importance of coordinating the work of organizational units
    D. number of first-line supervisors required

16. As part of his program to simplify clerical procedures, the chief of the records management division has decided to make an analysis of the forms used by his agency and to establish a system of forms control. He has assigned the assistant bureau chief to perform the bulk of the work in connection with this project. This assistant will receive part-time help from four subordinate employees.
    Of the following actions the bureau chief may take in planning the work on this project, the MOST appropriate one is for him to
    A. have the plans drawn up by the assistant and then submitted for final approval to the four part-time subordinates before work on the project is begun
    B. have the assistant work with him in drawing up the plans and then present the plans to the four part-time subordinates for their comments
    C. join with the five employees as a committee to formulate the plans for the project
    D. prepare the plans himself and then submit the plans for approval to all five employees who are to work on the project

17. Bureau X is composed of several clerical units, each supervised by a unit head accountable to the bureau chief. Assume that the bureau chief has a special task for an employee of one of the clerical units and wishes to issue instructions directly to the employee regarding this task.

The LEAST appropriate of the following procedures for the bureau chief to follow is to
- A. issue the instructions to the employee without notifying the employee's unit head
- B. give the instructions to the employee in the presence of the unit head
- C. ask the unit head to send the employee to him for instructions on this special task
- D. tell the employee to inform his unit head of the bureau chief's instructions

18. A bureau chief has scheduled a conference with the unit heads in his bureau to obtain their views on a major problem confronting the bureau.
The LEAST appropriate action for him to take in conducting this conference is to
    - A. present his own views of the solution of the problem before asking the unit heads for their opinions
    - B. call upon a participant in the conference for information which this participant should have as part of his job
    - C. weigh the opinions expressed at the conference in the light of the individual speaker's background and experience
    - D. summarize briefly at the conclusion of the conference, the important points covered and the conclusions reached

19. Of the following, the GREATEST stress in selecting employees for office supervisory positions should ordinarily be placed on
    - A. intelligence and educational background
    - B. knowledge of the work and capacity for leadership
    - C. sincere interest in the activities and objectives of the agency
    - D. skill in performing the type of work to be supervised

20. The MOST acceptable of the following guides in preparing the specifications for a form is that
    - A. when forms are to be printed on colored paper, the dark shades of colored paper should be used
    - B. *tumble* or *head-to-foot* should be used if forms printed on both sides of the sheet are to be placed in binders with side binding
    - C. provision for ballot-type entries should be made if items requiring *yes* or *no* entries are to appear on the form
    - D. all-rag ledger paper rather than all-wood pulp bond paper should be used for forms which will receive little handling and will be kept for a short time

21. Suppose you are the chief of a bureau which contains several operating units. On one occasion you observe one of your unit heads severely reprimand a subordinate for violating a staff regulation. This subordinate has a good record for observing staff regulations, and you believe the severe reprimand will seriously undermine the morale of the employee.
Of the following, the BEST action for you to take in this situation is to
    - A. call both the unit head and the subordinate into your office at the same time and have each present his views on the matter to you

B. refrain from intervening in this matter because the unit head may resent any interference
C. take the subordinate aside, inform him that the unit head had not intended to reprimand him several, and suggest that the matter be forgotten
D. discuss the matter with the unit head and suggest that he make some mitigating explanation to the subordinate

22. In addition to a report on its activities for the year, the one of the following items which it is MOST appropriate to include in an agency's annual report is
    A. praise for each of the accomplishments of the agency during the year
    B. pictures of agency personnel
    C. history of the agency
    D. descriptions of future activities and plans of the agency

23. Before transferring material from the active to the inactive files, the supervisor of the filing unit always consults the bureau heads directly concerned with the use of this material.
    This practice by the supervisor is
    A. *desirable*, chiefly because material that is no longer current for some bureaus may still be current for others
    B. *undesirable*, chiefly because it can only lead to disagreement among the bureau heads consulted
    C. *desirable*, chiefly because it is more economical to store records in transfer files than to keep them in the active files
    D. *undesirable*, chiefly because the filing supervisor is expected to make his own decision

24. The determination of essential factors in a specific kind of work and of qualifications of a worker necessary for its competent performance is MOST accurately defined as
    A. job analysis   B. micro-motion study
    C. cost analysis   D. production control

25. In the clinical approach to disciplinary problems, attention is focused on the basic causes of which the overt relations are merely symptomatic rather than on the specific violations which have brought the employee unfavorable notice.
    The MOST accurate implication of this quotation is that the clinical approach
    A. places emphasis on the actual violation rather than on the cause of the violation
    B. attempts to promote greater insight into the underlying factors which have led to the infractions
    C. does not evaluate the justness and utility of applying a specific penalty in a given situation
    D. avoids the necessity for disciplinarian action

26. The LEAST accurate of the following statements regarding the conduct of a conference is that
    A. when there is great disparity in the rank of the participants at a conference, the conference leader should ordinarily refrain from requesting an opinion point blank from a participant of relatively low rank
    B. when the aim of a conference is to obtain the opinion of a group of approximately the same rank, the rank of the conference leader should ordinarily not be too much higher than that of the participants
    C. in general, the chances that a conference will be fruitful are greatly increased if the conference leader's direct superior is one of the participants
    D. a top administrator invited to present a brief talk sponsoring a series of conferences for line supervisors should generally arrange to leave the conference as soon as appropriate after he has made his speech

27. In preparing a report for release to the general public, the bureau chief should GENERALLY present at the beginning of the report
    A. a description of the methods used in preparing the report
    B. anticipated criticism of the report and the answer to this criticism
    C. his conclusions and recommendations
    D. a bibliography of the sources used in preparing the report

28. Staff or functional supervision in an organization
    A. is least justified at the operational level
    B. is contrary to the principle of Unity of Command
    C. is more effective than authoritative supervision
    D. normally does not give the right to take direct disciplinary action

29. Suppose that you are the supervisor of Clerical Unit A in a city agency. Work processed in your unit is sent to Clerical Unit B for further processing. One of your subordinates complains to you that the supervisor of Clerical Unit B has been offering him unwarranted criticism of the method in which his work is performed.
    Of the following actions you may take, the MOST appropriate one for you to take FIRST is to
    A. request the supervisor of Clerical Unit B to meet with you and your subordinate to discuss this matter
    B. report this matter to this unit supervisor's immediate superior and request that this unsolicited criticism be discontinued
    C. obtain the facts from the subordinate and then discuss the matter with this unit supervisor
    D. tell your subordinate to refer the unit supervisor to you the next time he offers any criticism

30. This chart presents graphically a comparison of what is done and what is to be done. It is so ruled that each division of space represents both an amount of time and the quantity of work to be done during the particular unit of time. Horizontal lines drawn through these spaces show the relationship between the quantity of work actually done and that which is scheduled.

The chart referred to is known generally as a _____ chart.
  A. progress or Gantt   B. job correlation
  C. process or flow of work D. Simo work simplification

31. The personnel survey is a systematic and reasonably exhaustive analysis and statement of the facts and forces in an organization which affect the relations between employees and management, and between employees and their work, followed by recommendations as to ways of developing better personnel policies and procedures.
On the basis of this statement, it is LEAST accurate to state that one of the purposes served by a personnel survey is to
  A. appraise operating efficiency through an objective study of methods of production and a statistical interpretation of the facts
  B. set forth items and causes of poor morale in an inclusive way and in their proper perspective
  C. secure the facts to determine whether there is need of a more progressive personnel policy in an organization where personnel work is as yet undeveloped
  D. evaluate the effectiveness of a personnel policy where a progressive personnel policy is already in operation

31._____

32. It is generally recognized that there is a relationship between the size of an organization's staff, the number of supervisory levels, and the span of control (number of workers assigned to a supervisor).
The MOST accurate of the following statements regarding the relationship of these three elements is that if the size of
  A. an organization's staff should remain unchanged and the span of control should increase, then the number of supervisory levels would tend to increase
  B. the staff should decrease and the number of levels of supervision should increase, then the span of control would tend to decrease
  C. staff should increase and the number of supervisory levels should remain unchanged, then the span of control would tend to decrease
  D. staff should increase and the span of control should decrease, then the number of supervisory levels would tend to decrease

32._____

Questions 33-35.

DIRECTIONS: Questions 33 through 35 are to be answered on the basis of the organization chart shown on the next page. This chart presents the organizational structure of a division in a hypothetical agency. Each box designates a position in the organizational structure of this division. The symbol in each box represents the name of the individual occupying the position designated by the box. Thus, the name of the head of this division is represented by the symbol 1A.

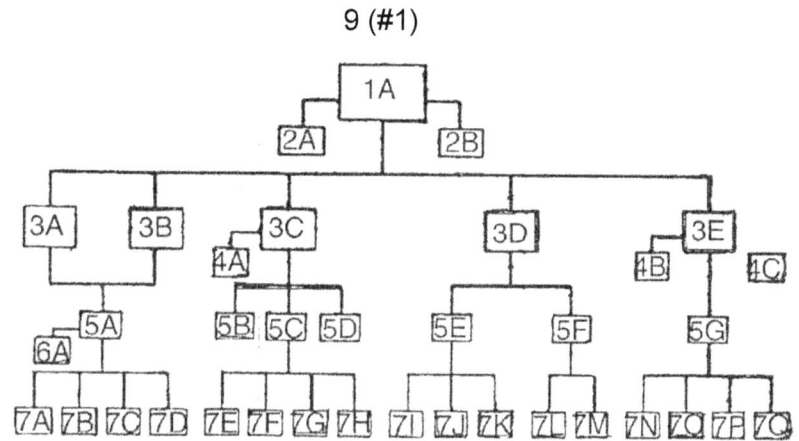

33. The one of the following who heads a subdivision which BEST illustrates in its organizational structure the characteristics of the pure line of organization is
 A. 3B B. 3C C. 3D D. 3E

34. The member of the organization who is MOST likely to receive conflicting orders because he is directly accountable to more than one superior is
 A. 5A B. 4A C. 5B D. 4C

35. Assume that 7K and 7P wish to exchange positions. Approval of this exchange must be obtained from each superior in the line of authority upward from 7K and from each superior in the line of authority extending upward from 7P.
The one of the following who is NOT in a line of authority extending upward from either 7K or 7P is
 A. 1A B. 3E C. 5F D. 3D

KEY (CORRECT ANSWERS)

1.	B	11.	D	21.	D	31.	A
2.	B	12.	C	22.	D	32.	B
3.	D	13.	B	23.	A	33.	C
4.	C	14.	A/C	24.	A	34.	A
5.	D	15.	B	25.	B	35.	C
6.	A	16.	B	26.	C		
7.	C	17.	A	27.	C		
8.	A	18.	A	28.	D		
9.	A	19.	B	29.	C		
10.	B	20.	C	30.	A		

TEST 2

DIRECTIONS: Each question or incomplete statement is followed by several suggested answers or completions. Select the one that BEST answers the question or completes the statement. *PRINT THE LETTER OF THE CORRECT ANSWER IN THE SPACE AT THE RIGHT.*

1. Analysis and simplification of office procedures are functions that should be conducted in all offices and on a continuing basis. These functions may be performed by the line supervisor, by staff methods specialists, or by outside consultants on methods analysis.
   An appraisal of these three methods of assigning responsibility for improving office procedures reveals that the LEAST accurate of the following statements is that
   A. outside consultants employed to simplify office procedures frequently bring with them a vast amount of previous experience as well as a fresh viewpoint
   B. line supervisors usually lack the special training which effective procedure analysis work requires
   C. continuity of effort and staff cooperation can better be secured by periodically employed consultants than by a permanent staff of methods analysts
   D. the reason line supervisors fail to keep procedures up to date is that the supervisor is too often overburdened with operating responsibilities

   1.____

2. A man cannot serve two masters.
   This statement emphasizes MOST the importance in an organization of
   A. span of control   B. specialization of work
   C. delegation of authority   D. unity of command

   2.____

3. An important aid in good office management is knowledge on the part of subordinates of the significance of their work.
   The possession of such knowledge by an employee will probably LEAST affect his
   A. interest in his work
   B. understanding of the relationship between the work of his unit and that of other units
   C. willingness to cooperate with other employees
   D. ability to undertake assignments requiring special skills

   3.____

4. For mediocre executives who do not have a flair for positive administration, the implantation in subordinates of anxiety about job retention is a safe, if somewhat unimaginative, method of insuring a modicum of efficiency in the working organization.
   Of the following, the MOST accurate statement according to this quotation is that
   A. implanting anxiety about job retention is a method usually employed by the mediocre executive to improve the efficiency of his organization

   4.____

B. an organization will operate with at least some efficiency if employees realize that unsatisfactory work performance may subject them to dismissal
C. successful executives with a flair for positive administration relieve their subordinates of any concern for their job security
D. the implantation of anxiety about job security in subordinates should not be used as a method of improving efficiency

5. Savings of 20 percent or more in clerical operating costs can often be achieved by improvement of the physical conditions under which office work is performed.
In general, the MOST valid of the following statements regarding physical conditions is that
   A. conference rooms should have more light than small rooms
   B. the tops of desks should be glossy rather than dull
   C. noise is reflected more by hard-surfaced materials than by soft or porous materials
   D. yellow is a more desirable wall color for offices receiving an abundance of sunlight than for offices receiving little sunlight

6. To the executive who directs the complex and diverse operations of large organizational unit, the conference is an important and, at times, indispensable tool of management. The inexperienced executive may, however, ploy the conference for a purpose for which it is ill fitted.
Of the following, the LEAST use of the conference by the executive is to
   A. reconcile conflicting views or interests
   B. develop an understanding by all concerned of a policy already adopted
   C. coordinate an activity involving several line supervisors
   D. perform technical research on a specific project

7. In planning the layout of office space, the office supervisor should bear in mind that one large room is a more efficient operating unit than the same number of square feet split up into smaller rooms.
Of the following, the LEAST valid basis for the preceding statement is that in the large room
   A. better light and ventilation are possible
   B. flow of work between employees is more direct
   C. supervision and control are more easily maintained
   D. time and motion studies are easier to conduct

8. The one of the following companies which is BEST known as a manufacturer of filing cabinets and office furniture is
   A. Pitney-Bowes, Inc.   B. Dennison Manufacturing Co.
   C. Wilson-Jones Co.   D. Shaw-Walker Co.

9. The program used to deliver audio-visual office presentations is known as
   A. PowerPoint   B. Excel   C. CGI   D. Dreamweaver

10. The principles of scientific office management are MOST frequently applied by government office supervisors in
    A. maintaining flexibility in hiring and firing
    B. developing improved pay scales
    C. standardizing clerical practices and procedures
    D. revising organizational structure

11. The one of the following factors to which the bureau head should attach LEAST importance in deciding on the advisability of substituting machine for manual operations in a given area of office work is the
    A. need for accuracy in the work
    B. relative importance of the work
    C. speed with which the work must be completed
    D. volume of work

12. The clerk displayed a *rudimentary* knowledge of the principles of supervision.
    The word *rudimentary* as used in this sentence means MOST NEARLY
    A. thorough   B. elementary   C. surprising   D. commendable

13. This is an *integral* part of our program.
    The word *integral* as used in this sentence means MOST NEARLY
    A. minor   B. unknown   C. essential   D. well-developed

14. A *contiguous* office is one that is
    A. spacious
    B. rectangular in shape
    C. adjoining
    D. crowded

15. This program was *sanctioned* by the department head.
    The word *sanctioned* as used in this sentence means MOST NEARLY
    A. devised   B. approved   C. modified   D. rejected

16. The file clerk performed his work in a *perfunctory* manner.
    The word *perfunctory* as used in this sentence means MOST NEARLY
    A. quiet   B. orderly   C. sullen   D. indifferent

17. He did not *impugn* the reasons given for the change in policy.
    The word *impugn* as used in this sentence means MOST NEARLY
    A. make insinuations against   B. verify in whole or part
    C. volunteer support for   D. overlook or ignore

18. The supervisor was unable to learn the identity of the *culpable* employee.
    The word *culpable* as used in this sentence means MOST NEARLY
    A. inaccurate   B. careless   C. guilty   D. dishonest

19. The announcement was made at a *propitious* time.
    The word *propitious* as used in this sentence means MOST NEARLY
    A. unexpected   B. busy   C. favorable   D. significant

20. He showed no *compunction* in carrying out this order.
    The word *compunction* as used in this sentence means MOST NEARLY
    A. feeling of remorse
    B. hesitation or delay
    C. tact or discretion
    D. disposition to please

21. He acted in a *fiduciary* capacity.
    The word *fiduciary* as used in this statement means MOST NEARLY
    A. administrative or executive in nature
    B. quasi-legal in nature
    C. involving confidence or trust
    D. requiring auditing or budgetary ability

22. To *temporize* means MOST NEARLY to
    A. allay temporarily the fears of
    B. render a temporary service
    C. yield temporarily to prevailing opinion
    D. react temperamentally

23. The new supervisor was *sanguine* about the prospects of success.
    The word *sanguine* as used in this sentence means MOST NEARLY
    A. uncertain   B. confident   C. pessimistic   D. excited

24. The supervisor was asked to *implement* the new policy.
    The word *implemented* as used in this sentence means MOST NEARLY
    A. explain
    B. revise
    C. delay the announcement of
    D. carry into effect

25. The word *intimation* means MOST NEARLY
    A. friendliness
    B. an attempt to frighten
    C. a difficult task
    D. an indirect suggestion

26. Mr. Jones has a *penchant* for this type of work
    The word *penchant* as used in this sentence means MOST NEARLY
    A. record of achievement
    B. unexplainable dislike
    C. lack of aptitude
    D. strong inclination

27. The speaker's comments were *desultory*.
    The word *desultory* as used in this sentence means MOST NEARLY
    A. inspiring   B. aimless   C. pertinent   D. rude

Questions 28-35.

DIRECTIONS: Questions 28 through 35 are to be answered SOLELY on the basis of the following chart which relates to the Investigation Division of Dept. X. This chart contains four curves which connect the points that show for each year the variations in percentage deviation from normal in the number of investigators, the number of clerical employee, the cost of personnel, and the number of cases processed for the period 2002-2012 inclusive. The year 2002 was designated as the normal year. The personnel of the Investigation Division consists of investigators and clerical employees only.

INVESTIGATION DIVISION, DEPARTMENT X

VARIATIONS IN NUMBER OF CASES PROCESSED, COST OF PERSONNEL
NUMBER OF CLERICAL EMPLOYEES, AND NUMBER OF INVESTIGATORS
FOR EACH YEAR FROM 2010 TO 2020 INCLUSIVE
(In percentages from normal)

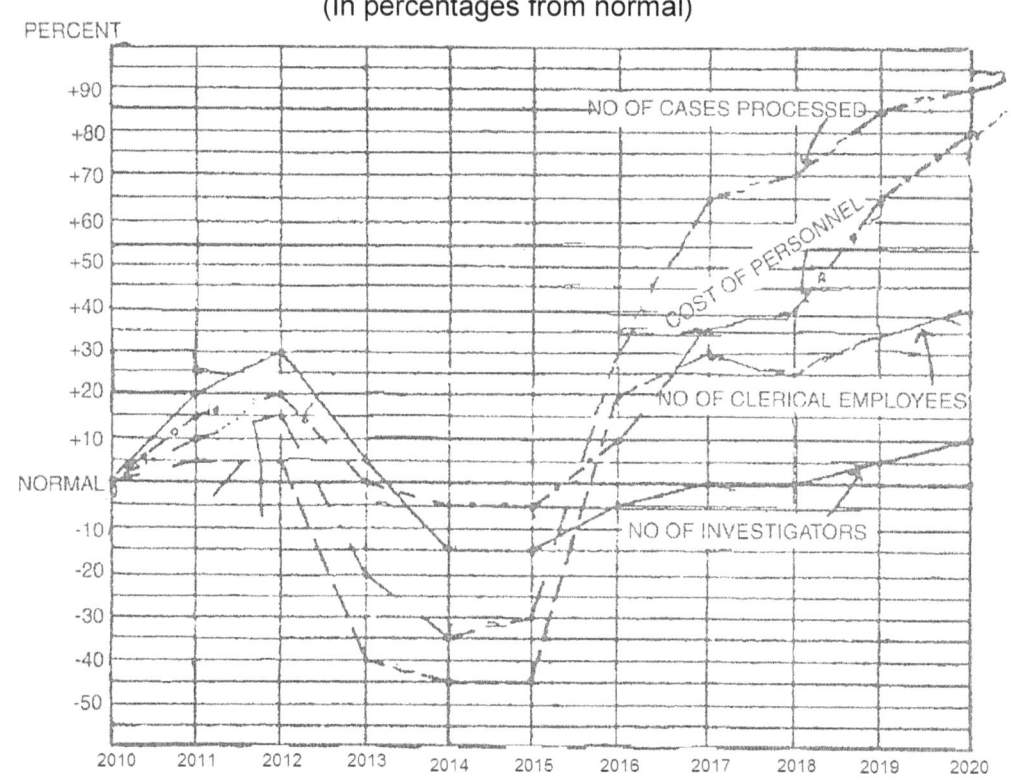

Example: If there were 80 clerical employees in the division in 2010 then the number of clerical employees in the division in 2017 was 104.

28. If 1,300 cases were processed by the division in 2014, then the number of cases processed in 2010 was   28._____
    A. 2,000   B. 1,755   C. 2,145   D. 1,650

6 (#2)

29. Of the following, the year in which there was no change in the size of the division's total staff from that of the preceding year is
    A. 2013   B. 2014   C. 2017   D. 2019

29.____

30. Of the following, the year in which the size of the division's staff decreased MOST sharply from that of the preceding year is
    A. 2013   B. 2014   C. 2015   D. 2016

30.____

31. An inspection of the chart discloses that the curve that fluctuates LEAST as determined by the average deviation from normal is the curve for the
    A. number of cases processed   B. cost of personnel
    C. number of clerical employees   D. number of investigators

31.____

32. A comparison of 2014 with 2020 reveals an increase in 2014 in the
    A. cost of personnel for the division
    B. number of cases processed per investigator
    C. number of cases processed per clerical employee
    D. number of clerical employees per investigator

32.____

33. If the personnel cost per case processed in 2010 was $12.30, then the personnel cost per case processed in 2020 was MOST NEARLY
    A. $9.85   B. $10.95   C. $11.65   D. $13.85

33.____

34. Suppose that there was a total of 108 employees in the division in 2010 and a total of 125 employees in 2018.
    On the basis of these figures, it is MOST accurate to state that the number of investigator employed in the division in 2018 was
    A. 40   B. 57   C. 68   D. 85

34.____

35. It is predicted that the number of cases processed in 2021 will exceed the number processed in 2010 by exactly the same quantity that the number processed in 2012 exceeded that processed in 2019. It is also predicted that the personnel cost in 2021 will exceed the personnel cost in 2020 by exactly the same amount that the 2020 personnel cost exceeded that for 2019. On the basis of these predictions, it is MOST accurate to state that the personnel cost per case in 2021 will be
    A. ten percent less than the personnel cost per case in 2020
    B. exactly the same as the personnel cost per case in 2020
    C. twice as much as the personnel cost per case in 2010
    D. exactly the same as the personnel cost per case in 2010

35.____

KEY (CORRECT ANSWERS)

1. C	11. B	21. C	31. D
2. D	12. B	22. C	32. C
3. D	13. C	23. B	33. C
4. B	14. C	24. D	34. A
5. C	15. B	25. B	35. D
6. D	16. D	26. D	
7. D	17. A	27. B	
8. D	18. C	28. A	
9. A	19. C	29. B	
10. C	20. A	30. A	

EXAMINATION SECTION

TEST 1

DIRECTIONS: Each question or incomplete statement is followed by several suggested answers or completions. Select the one that BEST answers the question or completes the statement. *PRINT THE LETTER OF THE CORRECT ANSWER IN THE SPACE AT THE RIGHT.*

1. The one of the following which BEST characterizes an agency in which delegation of authority is practiced on an organization-wide level is that the agency is
    A. autocratic
    B. authoritarian
    C. centralized
    D. decentralized

    1.____

2. The concept of the *chain of command* is MOST similar to which one of the following concepts?
    A. Span of control
    B. Matrix or task-force organization
    C. Scalar principle
    D. Functional departmentation

    2.____

3. The one of the following techniques which is NOT conducive to the establishment of an effective working relationship between employees and supervisors is
    A. periodic discussion of job performance with employees
    B. listening to employees when they discuss their job difficulties
    C. observation of employees on the job, in both individual and group situations, in order to help them with job performance
    D. treating all employees the same with respect to job performance and individual behavior

    3.____

4. Which of the following is a valid, commonly-raised objection to the establishment of work standards for office clerical workers?
    A. Routine clerical work is not subject to accurate measurement.
    B. Clerical work standards can only lower employee morale by creating undue pressure to produce work rapidly.
    C. Work standards are not effective tools for planning, scheduling, and routing clerical work.
    D. Some phases of many clerical jobs, such as telephone answering or information gathering, cannot be readily or accurately measured.

    4.____

5. Of the following, the feature which is LEAST characteristic of almost all successful staff relationships with line managers is that the staff employee
    A. is primarily a representative of his supervisor
    B. receives a salary at least equal to the average salary of his supervisor's direct line subordinates
    C. relies largely on persuasion to get his ideas put into effect
    D. is prepared to submerge his own personality and his own desire for recognition and see others often receive more recognition than he receives

    5.____

6. The one of the following systems which has, as its principal objective, the storage of items in files so that they may be readily found when needed is called
   A. information retrieval
   B. simulation
   C. critical path
   D. PERT

7. A detailed description of the steps to be taken in order to accomplish a job is MOST appropriately called a
   A. policy   B. rule   C. procedure   D. principle

8. In choosing the best place in the executive hierarchy to which to assign the task of making a certain type of decision, which one of the following should normally be LEAST important?
   A. Who knows the facts on which the decision will be based, or who can obtain them most readily?
   B. Who has the most adequate supply of current forms on which the decision is normally recorded?
   C. Who has the capacity to make sound decisions?
   D. How significant is the decision?

9. Of the following, the action which is LEAST likely to be either expressed or implied every time a manager delegates work to a subordinate is that the manager
   A. creates a need for a new class of positions
   B. indicates what work the subordinate is to do
   C. grants the subordinate some authority
   D. creates an obligation for the subordinate who accepts the work to try to complete it

10. Of the following, the LEAST appropriate use of organizational charts is to
    A. depict standard operating procedures
    B. indicate lines of responsibility
    C. indicate the relative level of key positions
    D. portray organizations graphically

11. The one of the following considerations which is generally LEAST important in deciding whether to automate a management operation by using a computer is whether the computer
    A. possesses a suitable array of programmed actions that might be taken
    B. can draw upon available data for information as to which alternative is best
    C. is already familiar to the staff of the organization
    D. can issue findings in a way that will facilitate the decision-making process

12. In evaluating a proposal to establish a library in your agency, it is generally considered LEAST necessary to determine
    A. the average time staff members spend on preparatory research when assigned to projects
    B. how often junior professional and technical staff members are sent out to *look something up* in a local library
    C. how much time and money agency executives devote to telephoning around the country seeking information before making decisions
    D. the quality of the research done by executives and scientists in the agency

13. In determining the number and type of tasks that should be combined into a single job, the one of the following which is normally the LEAST useful factor to consider is the
    A. benefit of functional specialization
    B. benefit of tall pyramid organization structures in increasing decentralization
    C. need for coordination of tasks with each other
    D. effect of the tasks assigned on the morale of the employee

14. Of the following, the one which is LEAST likely to be an objective of systems and procedures analysis is to
    A. eliminate as many unessential forms and records as feasible
    B. simplify forms in content and method of preparation
    C. mechanize repetitive, routine tasks
    D. expand as many of the forms as possible

15. A specific managerial function encompasses all of the following: The establishment of an intentional structure of roles through determination and enumeration of the activities required to achieve the goals of an enterprise and each part of it, the grouping of these activities, the assignment of such groups of activities to a manager, the delegation of authority to carry them out, and provision for coordination of authority and informational relationships horizontally and vertically in the organization structure.
    Of the following, the MOST appropriate term for this entire managerial function is
    A. organizing   B. directing   C. controlling   D. staffing

16. The optimum number of subordinates that a supervisor can supervise effectively generally tends to vary INVERSELY with the
    A. percentage of the supervisor's time devoted to supervision rather than operations
    B. repetition of activities
    C. degree of centralization of decision-making within the supervisor's unit
    D. ability of subordinates

17. Under certain circumstances, a top manager may desire to strengthen the position of his staff people by granting them concurring authority, so that no action may be taken in a functional area by subordinate line officials until a designated staff employee agrees to the action. For example, office manages may have to get the approval of the agency personnel officer before hiring a new employee.
This approach is likely to be MOST valid under which one of the following conditions?
    A. The top manager refrains from indicating the grounds on which the staff employee may grant or withhold his approval of line proposals.
    B. The point of view represented by the staff employee is particularly important, and the possible delay in action will not be serious.
    C. It is more important to fix specific accountability for failure to take appropriate action than for wrong actions taken.
    D. The top manager gives speed priority over prudence.

17.____

18. The inclusion of the reason why a superior in his written orders to his subordinates normally is MOST likely to
    A. encourage belief by the subordinates in the meaning and intent of the order
    B. be a waste of valuable time for both superior and subordinates
    C. be useful principally where the superior has no power to enforce the order
    D. discourage effective two-way communication between superior and subordinates

18.____

19. The one of the following which is generally LEAST justification for an administrator's search for alternative methods of attaining a given objective of the unit he heads is that such search
    A. always turns up a better method of attaining objectives than that currently in use
    B. helps to make certain that the best method has a chance to be found and evaluated
    C. helps to insure that his peers realize that the existing method of attaining the objective is not the best
    D. is a good way to train the unit's staff in the organization's operational procedures

19.____

20. *Managing-by-Objectives* tends to place PRINCIPAL emphasis upon which of the following?
    A. Use of primarily qualitative goals at all management levels
    B. Use of trait-appraisal systems based upon personality factors
    C. Use of primarily qualitative goals at lower management levels as contrasted with primarily quantitative goals at higher management levels
    D. Goals which are clear and verifiable

20.____

21. Which one of the following BEST identifies the two most important considerations which generally should determine the degree of management decentralization desirable in a given situation? The
    A. age of the subordinate executives to whom decisions may be delegated and the number of courses in management that they have completed
    B. number of skills and the competence possessed by subordinate executives and the distribution of the necessary information to the points of decision
    C. ratio of the salary of the superior executives to the salary of the subordinate executives and the number of titles on the executive staff
    D. number of titles in the executive staff and the distribution of information to those various titles

22. Which one of the following is generally LEAST likely to occur at mid-level management as a result of installing an electronic data processing system?
    A. The time that managers will be required to spend on the controlling function will increase.
    B. The number of contacts that managers will have with subordinates will increase.
    C. Additional time will be needed to train people for managerial positions.
    D. There will be an increase in the volume of information presented to managers for analysis.

23. The concept that the major source of managerial authority is derived from the subordinate's acceptance of the manager's power is MOST closely identified with
    A. Luther Gulick   B. John D. Mooney
    C. Frederick W. Taylor   D. Chester I. Barnard

24. The one of the following which is generally the principal objection to a pure *functional organization*, as compared with a pure *line organization*, is that
    A. there is a tendency to overload intermediate and supervisory management at each succeeding level of organization with wide and varied duties
    B. authority flows in an unbroken line from top management to the worker
    C. workers must often report to two or more supervisors
    D. there is a lack of specialization at the supervisory level

25. The appraisal of subordinates and their performance is an integral part of the supervisor's job. There is wide agreement that several basic principles must be taken into account by supervisors involved in the appraisal process in order to perform this function correctly.
    The one of the following statements which LEAST represents a basic principle of the appraisal process is:
    Appraisal(s)
    A. should be based more on performance of definite tasks than on personality considerations
    B. of long-range potential should rely most heavily on subjective judgment of that potential

C. involves the use of value judgments by the supervisor and does, therefore, require reference to pre-established standards
D. should aim at emphasizing subordinates' strengths rather than weaknesses

26. Of the following, the INITIAL step in the decision-making procedure normally is
    A. evaluation of alternatives
    B. implementing the chosen course of action
    C. listing potential solutions
    D. diagnosis and problem definition

27. Management textbooks are LEAST likely to define coordination as
    A. a concern for harmonious and unified action directed toward a common objective
    B. the essence of management, since the basic purpose of management is the achievement of harmony of individual effort toward the accomplishment of group goals
    C. the orderly arrangement of group effort to provide unity of action in pursuit of common purpose
    D. the transmittal of messages from senders to receivers, involving acts of persuasion of regulation, or simply the rendering of information

28. A number of important assumptions underlie the modern human relations approach to management and administration.
    The one of the following which is NOT an assumption integral to the human relations school of thought is that
    A. employee participation is essential to higher productivity
    B. employees are motivated solely by monetary factors
    C. teamwork is indispensable for organization growth and survival
    D. free-flow communications must be established and maintained for organizational effectiveness

29. Of the following, the MAIN purpose of systematic manpower planning is to
    A. analyze the levels of skill needed by each worker
    B. analyze causes of current vacancies, such as resignations, discharges, retirements, transfers, or promotions
    C. save money by eliminating useless jobs
    D. provide for the continuous and proper staffing of the workforce

30. A Planning-Programming-Budget System (PPBS) is PRIMARILY intended to do which of the following?
    A. Improve control through a budgeting-by-line-item system
    B. Plan and program budgets by objective rather than by function
    C. Raise money for social welfare programs
    D. Reduce budgets by planning and programming unspent funds

KEY (CORRECT ANSWERS)

1.	D	11.	C	21.	B
2.	C	12.	D	22.	A
3.	D	13.	B	23.	D
4.	D	14.	D	24.	C
5.	B	15.	A	25.	B
6.	A	16.	C	26.	D
7.	C	17.	B	27.	D
8.	B	18.	A	28.	B
9.	A	19.	B	29.	D
10.	A	20.	D	30.	B

TEST 2

DIRECTIONS: Each question or incomplete statement is followed by several suggested answers or completions. Select the one that BEST answers the question or completes the statement. *PRINT THE LETTER OF THE CORRECT ANSWER IN THE SPACE AT THE RIGHT.*

1. An administrative office is designed so that several administrative associates can log on to Microsoft Outlook and use an e-mail inbox that syncs in real time. Each associate can also send jobs to a central office printer. This is an example of
   A. network connectivity
   B. cloud connectivity
   C. office integration
   D. employee training

   1.____

2. In the planning of office space for the various bureaus and divisions of an agency, the one of the following arrangements which is generally considered to be MOST desirable in a conventional layout is to
   A. locate offices where employees do close and tedious work, such as accounting, and also offices of high-level executives away from windows so that distractions will be minimal
   B. locate *housekeeping* offices such as data processing and the mailroom very close to the high executive offices to increase convenience for the executives
   C. locate departments so that the work flow proceeds in an uninterrupted manner
   D. centralize the executive suite for maximum availability and public exposure

   2.____

3. Generally, the one of the following that is LEAST likely to be an essential step in a records retention plan is
   A. storing inactive records
   B. checking for accuracy of all records to be retained
   C. classification of all records
   D. making an inventory of all agency records

   3.____

4. The PRINCIPAL asset of an office layout diagram, as contrasted with the more abstract organization charts and flowcharts, is that an office layout diagram is
   A. more readily adaptable to strictly conceptual studies
   B. pictorial and therefore easier to understand
   C. suitable for showing both manual and machine processing operations, whereas organization charts and flowcharts may only be used for manual processing operations
   D. better suited for summarizing the number of work units produced at each step

   4.____

5. One of the assistants whom you supervise displays apparent familiarity toward a businessman who deals with your agency. This assistant spends more time with this person than the nature of his business would warrant, and you have observed that they are occasionally seen leaving the office together for lunch. In several instances, when this businessman comes into the office and this assistant is not at his desk, the businessman will not deal with any other staff member but will, instead, leave the office and return later when that particular employee is available.
Of the following courses of action, the FIRST one you should take is to
   A. audit the agency's books and records pertaining to this businessman
   B. rebuke the assistant for unprofessional conduct at the next staff meeting and warn him of disciplinary action if the practice is not discontinued forthwith
   C. advise your agency head of the action by the businessman and the assistant that has been described in the above paragraph
   D. reassign the assistant to duties that will not bring him into contact with any businessman

5.____

6. The one of the following factors which generally is the BEST justification for keeping higher inventories of supplies and equipment is an expected
   A. decline in demand
   B. price increase
   C. decline in prices
   D. increase in interest charges and storage costs

6.____

7. Statistical sampling is often used in administrative operations PRIMARILY because it enables
   A. administrators to determine the characteristics of appointed or elected officials
   B. decisions to be made based on mathematical and scientific fact
   C. courses of action to be determined by scientifically-based computer programs
   D. useful predictions to be made from relatively small samples

7.____

8. According to United States Department of Labor figures, the PRINCIPAL source of disabling injuries to office workers is
   A. flying objects and falling objects
   B. striking against equipment
   C. falls and slips
   D. handling materials

8.____

9. To expedite the processing of applications issued by your agency, you ask your assistant to design a form that will be used by your typists. After several discussions, he presents you with a draft that requires the typist to use 23 tabular-stop positions.
Such a form would PROBABLY be considered
   A. *undesirable*; typists would now have to soft-roll the platen to make the typing fall on the lines
   B. *desirable*; the fill-in operation by typists would be speeded up

9.____

C. *undesirable*; proper vertical alignment of data would be made difficult by the number of tabular-stop positions required
D. *desirable*; it would force the typists to utilize the tabular-stop device

Question 10.

DIRECTIONS: Following are five general instructions to file clerks which might appear in the proposed filing manual for an agency.

I. Follow instructions generally; if you have a suggestion for improvement in the filing methods, install it after notifying the file supervisor who will duly authorize a change in the manual.
II. You may discuss the contents of files with fellow employees or outsiders, but do NOT give papers from the file to any person whose duties have no relation to the material requested.
III. All special instructions must be given by the file supervisor. Any problems that arise outside the regular routine of filing must be decided by the file supervisor, not by a fellow clerk.
IV. You will not be held responsible for your own errors; thus, refrain from asking other workers for instructions. No one is more interested in helping you in your training than your file supervisor.
V. Speed is the first essential in filing; make it your primary consideration—quick finding of filed material is the real test of your efficiency.

10. Which of the choices listed below BEST identifies those of the above statements that should or should not be followed by agencies in the functioning of their filing sections?
Instruction(s) _____ should be followed; instructions _____ should not be followed.
A. I, II, III; IV, V
B. III; I, II, IV, V
C. II, IV; I, III, V
D. I, III; II, IV, V

11. Listed below are five steps in the process of staffing:
I. Authorization for staffing
II. Manpower planning
III. Development of applicant sources
IV. Evaluation of applicants
V. Employment decisions and offers
The one of the following sequences which is generally the MOST logical arrangement of the above steps is:
A. I, II, III, IV, V
B. II, I, III, IV, V
C. III, I, II, IV, V
D. II, III, I, IV, V

12. Job enrichment is LEAST likely to lead to
A. fewer employee grievances
B. increased employee productivity
C. people acting as adjuncts of increased automation
D. increased employee morale

13. Of the following, programmed instruction would usually be MOST effective in teaching
    A. principles of decision-making
    B. technical skills and knowledge
    C. good judgment
    D. executive management ability

14. Assume that a group has been working effectively with a contributing nonconformist in its midst.
    The BEST of the following reasons for the group to retain the nonconformist generally is that
    A. nonconformists stimulate groups to think
    B. he may be their boss some day
    C. nonconformists usually are fun to work with
    D. another nonconformist will usurp his role

15. The *grievance-arbitration* process involves systematic union-management deliberation regarding a complaint that work- or contract-related.
    An outcome that does NOT result from this process is
    A. a communications channel from the rank-and-file workers to higher management is developed or improved
    B. the contract is immediately changed to provide justice for both parties
    C. both labor and management identify those parts of the contract that need to be clarified and modified in subsequent negotiations
    D. the language of the agreement is informally translated into understandable terms for the parties bound by it

16. In government, job evaluation is the process of determining the relative worth of the various jobs in an organization so that differential wages can be paid. Job evaluation is based on several basic assumptions.
    Of the assumptions listed below, the MOST questionable is that
    A. the cash payments in government should be substantially higher than those in local private industry
    B. it is logical to pay the most for jobs that contribute most to the organization
    C. people feel more fairly treated if wages are based on the relative worth of their jobs
    D. the best way to achieve the goals of the enterprise is to maintain a wage structure based on job worth

17. Of the following, the training method that normally provides the instructor with the LEAST *feedback* from the trainees is
    A. the lecture method
    B. the conference method
    C. simulation or gaming techniques
    D. seminar instruction

18. Insufficient and inappropriate delegation of work assignments is MOST often the fault of
    A. subordinates who are unwilling to accept responsibility for their own mistakes
    B. a paternal attitude on the part of management

C. the immediate supervisor
D. subordinates who are too willing to take on extra responsibility

19. As contrasted with expense budgets, capital budgets are MORE likely to
    A. be used for construction of physical facilities
    B. be designed for a shorter time period
    C. include personal service expenditures
    D. include fringe benefits

19.____

20. During the first quarter of a year, a division's production rate was 1.26 man-hours per work unit produced. For the second quarter of that year, all other factors (e.g., size of staff, character of work unit, etc.) remained constant, except that the manner of reporting production rate was changed to work units per man-hour instead of man-hours per work unit. During that second quarter, the unit's production rate was .89 work units per man-hour.
    On the basis of the above information, it would be MOST NEARLY CORRECT to conclude that the division's production rate during the second quarter was approximately _____ than during the first quarter.
    A. 30% lower   B. 10% lower   C. 10% higher   D. 30% higher

20.____

Questions 21-22.

DIRECTIONS: Questions 21 and 22 are to be answered on the basis of the following information.

The five bureaus within a department sent the following budget requests to the department head:
Bureau A: $10 million
Bureau B: $12 million
Bureau C: $18 million
Bureau D: $6 million
Bureau E: $4 million

After reviewing all of these requests, the department head decided to reduce these requests so that they would total only $40 million. He considered the following two options to accomplish this:

Option I: Reduce the requests of Bureaus A, B, and D by an equal dollar amount. Reduce the dollar amount request of Bureau C by 2½ times the dollar amount that he reduces the request of Bureau B. Reduce the dollar amount request of Bureau E by ½ of the dollar amount that he reduces the request of Bureau B.

Option II: First, reduce the dollar amount request of all five bureaus by 15%. Then, the remaining reduction required by the entire department would be achieved by further reducing the resulting budget requests of Bureaus B and C by an equal dollar amount each.

21. Under Option I, the dollar amount request for Bureau E, after reduction by the department head, would be MOST NEARLY _____ millions.
    A. $1²/₃   B. $2¹/₃   C. $3¹/₆   D. $3½

22. Under Option II, the dollar amount of the request of Bureau B, after both reductions were made by the department head, would be MOST NEARLY _____ millions.
    A. $8   B. $9   C. $10   D. $11

23. The Summary of finding of a long management report intended for typical manager should generally appear _____ the report.
    A. at the very beginning of
    B. at the end of the report
    C. throughout
    D. in the middle of

24. Of the following, the BIGGEST disadvantage in allowing a free flow of communications in an agency is that such a free flow
    A. decreases creativity
    B. increases the use of the *grapevine*
    C. lengthens the chain of command
    D. reduces the executive's power to direct the flow of information

25. A downward flow of authority in an organization is one example of _____ communications.
    A. horizontal   B. informal   C. circular   D. vertical

26. Workers who belong to a cohesive group are generally thought to
    A. have more job-related anxieties than those who do not
    B. be less well-adjusted than those who do not
    C. derive little satisfaction from the group
    D. Conform to group norms more closely than those in noncohesive groups

27. The one of the following which BEST exemplifies negative motivation is
    A. a feeling on the part of the worker that the work is significant
    B. monetary rewards offered the worker for high levels of output
    C. reducing or withholding the worker's incentive rewards when performance is mediocre
    D. nonmonetary rewards given the worker, such as publicizing a good suggestion

28. Of the following, the one that would be MOST likely to block effective communication is
    A. concentration only on the issues at hand
    B. lack of interest or commitment
    C. use of written reports
    D. use of charts and graphs

29. Many functions formerly centralized in a department of personnel have been decentralized, in whole or in part, to operating agencies.
The one of the following personnel functions which has been LEAST decentralized is
   A. positive evaluation
   B. investigation of non-competitive employees
   C. investigation of competitive employees
   D. jurisdictional classification

30. In making a position analysis for a duties classification, the one of the following factors which MUST be considered is the _____ the incumbent.
   A. capabilities of
   B. qualifications of
   C. efficiency attained by
   D. responsibility assigned to

KEY (CORRECT ANSWERS)

1.	A	11.	B	21.	C
2.	C	12.	C	22.	B
3.	B	13.	B	23.	A
4.	B	14.	A	24.	D
5.	C	15.	B	25.	D
6.	B	16.	A	26.	D
7.	D	17.	A	27.	C
8.	C	18.	C	28.	B
9.	C	19.	A	29.	D
10.	B	20.	C	30.	D

EXAMINATION SECTION
TEST 1

DIRECTIONS: Each question or incomplete statement is followed by several suggested answers or completions. Select the one that BEST answers the question or completes the statement. *PRINT THE LETTER OF THE CORRECT ANSWER IN THE SPACE AT THE RIGHT.*

1. When a supervisor in a large office introduces a change in the regular office procedure, it is USUAL to expect
   A. immediate acceptance by office staff, unless the change is unnecessary
   B. an immediate production increase, since new procedures are more stimulating than old ones
   C. a temporary production loss, even if the change is really an overall improvement
   D. resistance to the change only if it has been put into writing

   1.____

2. A supervisor evaluates the performance of subordinates and then applies measures, where needed, which result in bringing performance up to desired standards.
   Which of the following functions of management might he BEST be described as performing?
   A. Organizing   B. Controlling   C. Directing   D. Planning

   2.____

3. Assume that, as a supervisor, you have been assigned responsibility for a new and complex project which entails collection and analysis of data. You have prepared general written instructions which explain the project and procedures to be followed by several statisticians.
   Which of the following procedures would be MOST advisable for you, as the supervisor, to follow?
   A. Distribute the instructions to your subordinates to come to you with any important questions
   B. Distribute the instructions and advise subordinates to come to you with any important questions
   C. Meet with subordinates as a group and explain the project using the written instructions as a handout
   D. Delegate responsibility for further explanation of the project to an immediate qualified subordinate to free you for concentration on research design

   3.____

4. Supervisors have an obligation to make careful and thorough appraisals and reports of probationary employees.
   Of the following, the MOST important justification for this statement is that the probationary period
   A. should be used for positive development of the employee's understanding of the organization
   B. is the most effective period for changing a new employee's knowledges, skills, and attitudes

   4.____

C. insures that the employee will meet work standard requirements on future assignments
D. should be considered as the final step in the selection process

5. Many studies of management indicate that a principal reason for failure of supervisors lies in their ability to delegate duties effectively.
Which one of the following practices by a supervisor would NOT be a block to successful delegation?
   A. Instructing the delegate to follow a set procedure in carrying out the assignment
   B. Maintaining point-by-point control over the process delegated
   C. Transferring ultimate responsibility for the duties assigned to the delegate
   D. Requiring the delegate to keep the delegator informed of his progress

6. Crosswise communication occurs between personnel at lower or middle levels of different organizational units. It often speeds information and improves understanding, but has certain dangers.
Of the following proposed policies, which would NOT be important as a safeguard in crosswise communication?
   A. Supervisors should agree as to how crosswise communication should occur.
   B. Crosswise relationships must exist only between employees of equal status.
   C. Subordinates must keep their superiors informed about their interdepartmental communications.
   D. Subordinates must refrain from making commitments beyond their authority.

7. Systems theory has given us certain principles which are as applicable to organizational and social activities as they are to those of science.
With regard to the training of employees in an organization, which of the following is likely to be MOST consistent with the modern systems approach? Training can be effective ONLY when it is
   A. related to the individual abilities of the employees
   B. done on all levels of the organizational hierarchy
   C. evaluated on the basis of experimental and control groups
   D. provided on the job by the immediate supervisor

8. The management of a large agency, before making a decision as to whether or not to computerize its operations, should have a feasibility study made.
Of the following, the one which is LEAST important to include in such a study is
   A. the current abilities of management and staff to use a computer
   B. projected workloads and changes in objectives of functional units in the agency
   C. the contributions expected of each organizational unit towards achievement of agency objectives
   D. the decision-making activity and informational needs of each management function

9. Managing information covers the creation, collection, processing, storage, and transmission of information that appears in a variety of forms. A supervisor responsible for a statistical unit can be considered, in many respects, an information manager.
   Of the following, which would be considered the LEAST important aspect of the information manager's job?
   A. Establishing better information standards and forms
   B. Reducing the amount of unnecessary paperwork performed
   C. Producing progressively greater numbers of informational reports
   D. Developing a greater appreciation for information among management members

10. Because of the need for improvement in information systems throughout industry and government, various techniques for improving these systems have been developed.
    Of these, *systems simulation* is a technique for improving systems which
    A. creates new ideas and concepts through the use of a computer
    B. deals with time controlling of interrelated systems which make up an overall project
    C. permits experimentation with various ideas to see what results might be obtained
    D. does not rely on assumptions which condition the value of the results

11. The one of the following which it is NOT advisable for a supervisor to do when dealing with individual employees is to
    A. recognize a person's outstanding service as well as his mistakes
    B. help an employee satisfy his need to excel
    C. encourage an efficient employee to seek better opportunities even if this action may cause the supervisor to lose a good worker
    D. take public notice of an employee's mistakes so that fewer errors will be made in the future

12. Suppose that you are in a department where you are given the responsibility for teaching seven new assistants a number of routine procedures that all assistants should know.
    Of the following, the BEST method for you to follow in teaching these procedures is to
    A. separate the slower learners from the faster learners and adapt your presentation to their level of ability
    B. instruct all the new employees in a group without attempting to assess differences in learning rates
    C. restrict your approach to giving them detailed written instructions in order to save time
    D. avoid giving the employees written instructions in order to force them to memorize job procedures quickly

13. Suppose that you are a supervisor to whom several assistants must hand in work for review. You notice that one of the assistants gets very upset whenever you discover an error in his work, although all the assistants make mistakes from time to time.
    Of the following, it would be BEST for you to
    A. arrange discreetly for the employee's work to be reviewed by another supervisor
    B. ignore his reaction since giving attention to such behavior increases its intensity
    C. suggest that the employee seek medical help since he has such great difficulty in accepting normal criticism
    D. try to build the employee's self-confidence by emphasizing those parts of his work that are done well

14. Suppose you are a supervisor responsible for supervising a number of assistants in an agency where each assistant receives a manual of policies and procedures when he first reports for work. You have been asked to teach your subordinates a new procedure which requires knowledge of several items of policy and procedure found in the manual.
    The one of the following techniques which it would be BEST for you to employ is to
    A. give verbal instructions which include a review of the appropriate standard procedures as well as an explanation of new tasks
    B. give individual instruction restricted to the new procedure to each assistant as the need arises
    C. provide written instructions for new procedural elements and refer employees to their manuals for explanation of standard procedures
    D. ask employees to review appropriate sections of their manual and then explain those aspects of the new procedure which the manual did not cover

15. Supposes that you are a supervisor in charge of a unit in which changes in work procedures are about to be instituted.
    The one of the following which you, as the supervisor, should anticipate as being MOST likely to occur during the changeover is
    A. a temporary rise in production because of interest in the new procedures
    B. uniform acceptance of these procedures on the part of your staff
    C. varying interpretations of the new procedures by your staff
    D. general agreement among staff members that the new procedures are advantageous

16. Suppose that a supervisor and one of the assistants under his supervision are known to be friends who play golf together on weekends.
    The maintenance of such a friendship on the part of the supervisor is GENERALLY
    A. *acceptable* as long as this assistant continues to perform his duties satisfactorily
    B. *unacceptable* since the supervisor will find it difficult to treat the assistant as a subordinate

C. *acceptable* if the supervisor does not favor this assistant above other employees
D. *unacceptable* because the other assistants will resent the friendship regardless of the supervisor's behavior on the job

17. Suppose that you are a supervisor assigned to review the financial records of an agency which has recently undergone a major reorganization.
Which of the following would it be BEST for you to do FIRST?
    A. Interview the individual in charge of agency financial operations to determine whether the organizational changes affect the system of financial review
    B. Discuss the nature of the reorganization with your own supervisor to anticipate and plan a new financial review procedure
    C. Carry out the financial review as usual, and adjust your methods to any problems arising from the reorganization
    D. Request a written report from the agency head explaining the nature of the reorganization and recommending changes in the system of financial review

17.____

18. Suppose that a newly assigned supervisor finds that he must delegate some of his duties to subordinates in order to get the work done.
Which one of the following would NOT be a block to his delegating these duties effectively?
    A. Inability to give proper directions as to what he wants done
    B. Reluctance to take calculated risks
    C. Lack of trust in his subordinates
    D. Retaining ultimate responsibility for the delegated work

18.____

19. A supervisor sometimes performs the staff function of preparing and circulating reports among bureau chiefs.
Which of the following is LEAST important as an objective in designing and writing such reports?
    A. Providing relevant information on past, present, and future actions
    B. Modifying his language in order to insure goodwill among the bureau chiefs
    C. Helping the readers of the report to make appropriate decisions
    D. Summarizing important information to help readers see trends or outstanding points

19.____

20. Suppose you are a supervisor assigned to prepare a report to be read by all bureau chiefs in your agency.
The MOST important reason for avoiding highly technical accounting terminology in writing this report is to
    A. ensure the accuracy and relevancy of the text
    B. insure winning the readers' cooperation
    C. make the report more interesting to the readers
    D. make it easier for the readers to understand

20.____

21. Which of the following conditions is MOST likely to cause low morale in an office?
    A. Different standards of performance for individuals in the same title
    B. A requirement that employees perform at full capacity
    C. Standards of performance that vary with titles of employees
    D. Careful attention to the image of the division or department

22. A wise supervisor or representative of management realizes that, in the relationship between supervisor and subordinates, all power is not on the side of management, and that subordinates do sometimes react to restrictive authority in such a manner as to seriously retard management's objectives. A wise supervisor does not stimulate such reactions.
    In the subordinate's attempt to retaliate against an unusually authoritative management style, which of the following actions would generally be LEAST successful for the subordinate? He
    A. joins with other employees in organizations to deal with management
    B. obviously delays in carrying out instructions which are given in an arrogant or incisive manner
    C. performs assignments exactly as instructed even when he recognizes errors in instructions
    D. holds back the flow of feedback information to superiors

23. Which of the following is the MOST likely and costly effect of vague and indefinite instructions given to subordinates by a supervisor?
    A. Misunderstanding and ineffective work on the part of the subordinates
    B. A necessity for the supervisor to report identical instructions with each assignment
    C. A failure of the supervisor to adequately keep the attention of subordinates
    D. Inability of subordinates to assist each other in the absence of the supervisor

24. At the professional level, there is a kind of informal authority which exercises itself even though no delegation of authority has taken place from higher management. It occurs within the context of knowledge required and professional competence in a special area.
    An example of the kind of authority described in this statement is MOST clearly exemplified in the situation where a senior supervisor influences associates and subordinates by virtue of the
    A. salary level fixed for his particular set of duties
    B. amount of college training he possesses
    C. technical position he has gained and holds on the work team
    D. initiative and judgment he has demonstrated to his supervisor

25. An assistant under your supervision attempts to conceal the fact that he has made an error.
    Under this circumstance, it would be BEST for you, as the supervisor, to proceed on the assumption that

A. this evasion indicates something wrong in the fundamental relationship between you and the assistant
B. this evasion is not deliberate, if the error is subsequently corrected by the assistant
C. this evasion should be overlooked if the error is not significant
D. detection and correction of errors will come about as an automatic consequence of internal control procedures

KEY (CORRECT ANSWERS)

1.	C	11.	D
2.	B	12.	B
3.	C	13.	D
4.	D	14.	A
5.	D	15.	C
6.	B	16.	C
7.	B	17.	A
8.	A	18.	D
9.	C	19.	B
10.	C	20.	D

21. A
22. B
23. A
24. C
25. A

TEST 2

DIRECTIONS: Each question or incomplete statement is followed by several suggested answers or completions. Select the one that BEST answers the question or completes the statement. *PRINT THE LETTER OF THE CORRECT ANSWER IN THE SPACE AT THE RIGHT.*

1. The unit which you supervise has a number of attorneys, accountants, examiners, statisticians, and clerks who prepare some of the routine papers required to be filed. In order to be certain that nothing goes out of your office that is improper, you have instituted a system that requires that you review and initial all moving papers, memoranda of law and briefs that are prepared. As a result, you put in a great deal of overtime and even must take work home with you frequently.
   A situation such as this is
   A. inevitable if you are to keep proper controls over the quality of the office work product
   B. indicative of the fact that the agency must provide an additional position within your office for an assistant supervisor who would do all the reviewing, leaving you free for other pressing administrative work and to handle the most difficult work in your unit
   C. the logical result of an ever-increasing caseload
   D. symptomatic of poor supervision and management

1.____

2. Your unit has been assigned a new employee who has never worked for the city.
   To orient him to his job in your unit, of the following, the BEST procedure is first to
   A. assign him to another employee to whatever work that employee gives him so that he can become familiar with your work and at the same time be productive
   B. give him copies of the charter and code provisions affecting your operations plus any in-office memoranda or instructions that are available and have him read them
   C. assign him to work on a relatively simple problem and then, after he has finished it, tell him politely what he did wrong
   D. explain to him the duties of his position and the functions of the office

2.____

3. A bureau chief who supervises other supervisors makes it a practice to assign them more cases than they can possibly handle.
   This approach is
   A. *right*, because it results in getting more work done than would otherwise be the case
   B. *right*, because it relieves the bureau chief making the assignments of the responsibility of getting the work done
   C. *wrong*, because it builds resistance on the part of those called upon to handle the caseload
   D. *wrong*, because superiors lose track of cases

3.____

4. Assume you are a supervisor and are expected to exercise *authority* over subordinates.
   Which of the following BEST defines *authority*? The
   A. ability to control the nature of the contribution a subordinate is desirous of making
   B. innate inability to get others to do for you what you want to get done irrespective of their own wishes
   C. legal right conferred by the agency to control the actions of others
   D. power to determine a subordinate's attitude toward his agency and his superiors

4.____

5. Paternalistic leadership stresses a paternal or fatherly influence in the relationships between the leader and the group and is manifest in a watchful care for the comfort and welfare of the followers.
   Which one of the following statements regarding paternalistic leadership is MOST accurate?
   A. Employees who work well under paternalistic leadership come to expect such leadership even when the paternal leader has left the organization.
   B. Most disputes arising out of supervisor-subordinate relationships develop because group leaders do not understand the principles of paternalistic leadership.
   C. Paternalistic leadership frequently destroys office relationships because most employees are turned into non-thinking dependent robots.
   D. Paternalistic leadership is rarely, if ever, successful because employees resent paternalistic leadership which they equate with weakness.

5.____

6. Employees who have extensive dealings with members of the public should have, as much as possible, *real acceptance* of all people and a willingness to serve everyone impartially and objectively.
   Assuming that this statement is correct, the one of the following which would be the BEST demonstration of *real acceptance* is
   A. condoning antisocial behavior
   B. giving the appearance of agreeing with everyone encountered
   C. refusing to give opinions on anyone's behavior
   D. understanding the feelings expressed through a person's behavior

6.____

7. Assume that the agency chief has requested you to help plan a public relations program because of recent complaints from citizens about the unbecoming conduct and language of various groups of city employees who have dealings with the public.
   In carrying out this assignment, the one of the following steps which should be undertaken FIRST is to
   A. study the characteristics of the public clientele dealt with by employees in your agency
   B. arrange to have employees attend several seminars on human relations
   C. develop several procedures for dealing with the public and allow the staff to choose the one which is best
   D. find out whether the employees in your agency may oppose any plan proposed by you

7.____

8. The one of the following statements which BEST expresses the relationship between the morale of government employees and the public relations aspects of their work is:
   A. There is little relationship between employee morale and public relations, chiefly because public opinion is shaped primarily by response to departmental policy formulation.
   B. Employee morale is closely related to public relations, chiefly because the employee's morale will largely determine the manner in which he deals with the public.
   C. There is little relationship between employee morale and public relations, chiefly because public relations is primarily a function of the agency's public relations department.
   D. Employee morale is closely related to public relations, chiefly because employee morale indicates the attitude of the agency's top officials toward the public.

9. As a supervisor, you are required to deal extensively with the public. The agency chief has indicated that he is considering holding a special in-service training course for employees in communications skills
   Holding this training course would be
   A. *advisable*, chiefly because government employees should receive formal training in public relations skills
   B. *inadvisable*, chiefly because the public regards such training as a *waste of the taxpayers money*
   C. *advisable*, chiefly because such training will enable the employee to aid in drafting departmental press releases
   D. *inadvisable*, chiefly because of the great difficulty involved in developing skills through formal instruction

10. Assume that you have extensive contact with the public. In dealing with the public, sensitivity to an individual's attitudes is important because these attitudes can be used to predict behavior.
    However, the MAIN reason that attitudes CANNOT successfully predict all behavior is that
    A. attitudes are highly resistant to change
    B. an individual acquires attitudes as a function of growing up in a particular cultural environment
    C. attitudes are only one of many factors which determine a person's behavior
    D. an individual's behavior is not always observable

11. Rotation of employees from assignment to assignment is sometimes advocated by management experts.
    Of the following, the MOST probable advantage to the organization of this practice is that it leads to
    A. higher specialization of duties so that excessive identification with the overall organization is reduced
    B. increased loyalty of employees to their immediate supervisors

C. greater training and development of employees
D. intensified desire of employees to obtain additional, outside formal education

12. Usually, a supervisor should attempt to standardize the work for which he is responsible.
The one of the following which is a BASIC reason for doing this is to
   A. eliminate the need to establish priorities
   B. permit the granting of exceptions to rules and special circumstances
   C. facilitate the taking of action based on applicable standards
   D. learn the identity of outstanding employees

12.____

13. The differences between line and staff authority are often quite ambiguous.
Of the following, the ESSENTIAL difference is that
   A. *line authority* is exercised by first-level supervisors; *staff authority* is exercised by higher-level supervisors and managerial staff
   B. *staff authority* is the right to issue directives; *line authority* is entirely consultative
   C. *line authority* is the power to make decisions regarding intra-agency matters; *staff authority* involves decisions regarding inter-agency matters
   D. *staff authority* is largely advisory; *line authority* is the right to command

13.____

14. Modern management theory stresses work-centered motivation as one way of increasing the productivity of employees.
The one of the following which is PARTICULARLY characteristic of such motivation is that it
   A. emphasizes the crucial role of routinization of procedures
   B. stresses the satisfaction to be found in performing work
   C. features the value of wages and fringe benefits
   D. uses a firm but fair method of discipline

14.____

15. The agency's informal communications network is called the *grapevine*.
If employees are learning about important organizational developments primarily through the grapevine, this is MOST likely an indication that
   A. official channels of communication are not functioning so efficiently as they should
   B. supervisory personnel are making effective use of the grapevine to communicate with subordinates
   C. employees already have a clear understanding of the agency's policies and procedures
   D. upward formal channels of communication within the agency are informing management of employee grievances

15.____

16. Of the following, a flow chart is BEST described as a chart which shows
   A. the places through which work moves in the course of the job process
   B. which employees perform specific functions leading to the completion of a job

16.____

C. the schedules for production and how they eliminate waiting time between jobs
D. how work units are affected by the actions of related work units

17. Evaluation of the results of training is necessary in order to assess its value. Of the following, the BEST technique for the supervisor to use in determining whether the training under consideration actually resulted in the desired modification of the behavior of the employee concerned is through
    A. inference   B. job analysis   C. observation   D. simulation

17.____

18. The usual distinction between line and staff authority is that staff authority is mainly advisory, whereas line authority is the right to command. However, a third category has been suggested-prescriptive-to distinguish those personnel whose functions may be formally defined as staff but in practice exercise considerable authority regarding decisions relating to their specialties.
    The one of the following which indicates the MAJOR purpose of creating this third category is to
    A. develop the ability of each employee to perform a greater number of tasks
    B. reduce line-staff conflict
    C. prevent over-specialization of functions
    D. encourage decision-making by line personnel

18.____

19. It is sometimes considered desirable to train employees to a standard of proficiency higher than that deemed necessary for actual job performance. The MOST likely reason for such overtraining would be to
    A. eliminate the need for standards
    B. increase the value of refresher training
    C. compensate for previous lack of training
    D. reduce forgetting or loss of skill

19.____

20. Assume that you have been directed to immediately institute various new procedures in the handling of records.
    Of the following, the BEST method for you to use to insure that your subordinates know exactly what to do is to
    A. circulate a memorandum explaining the new procedure have your subordinates initial it
    B. explain the new procedures to one or two subordinates and ask them to tell the others
    C. have a meeting with your subordinates to give them copies of the procedures and discuss it with them
    D. post the new procedures where they can be referred to by all those concerned

20.____

6 (#2)

21. A supervisor decided to hold a problem-solving conference with his entire staff and distributed an announcement and agenda one week before the meeting.
Of the following, the BEST reason for providing each participant with an agenda is that
   A. participants will feel that something will be accomplished
   B. participants may prepare for the conference
   C. controversy will be reduced
   D. the top man should state the expected conclusions

21._____

22. In attempting to motivate employees, rewards are considered preferable to punishment PRIMARILY because
   A. punishment seldom has any effect on human behavior
   B. punishment usually results in decreased production
   C. supervisors find it difficult to punish
   D. rewards are more likely to result in willing cooperation

22._____

23. In an attempt to combat the low morale in his organization, a high-level supervisor publicized an *open-door* policy to allow employees who wished to do so to come to him with their complaints.
Which of the following is LEAST likely to account for the fact that no employee came in with a complaint?
   A. Employees are generally reluctant to go over the heads of their immediate supervisors.
   B. The employees did not feel that management would help them.
   C. The low morale was not due to complaints association with the job
   D. The employees felt that they had more to lose than to gain.

23._____

24. It is MOST desirable to use written instructions rather than oral instructions for a particular job when
   A. a mistake on the job will not be serious
   B. the job can be completed in a short time
   C. there is no need to explain the job minutely
   D. the job involves many details

24._____

25. You have been asked to prepare for public distribution a statement dealing with a controversial matter.
Of the following approaches, the one which would usually be MOST effective is to present your department's point of view
   A. as tersely as possible with no reference to any other matters
   B. developed from ideas and facts well known to most readers
   C. and show all the statistical data and techniques which were used in arriving at it
   D. in such a way that the controversial parts are omitted

25._____

KEY (CORRECT ANSWERS)

1. D
2. D
3. C
4. C
5. A

6. D
7. A
8. B
9. A
10. C

11. C
12. C
13. D
14. B
15. A

16. A
17. C
18. B
19. D
20. C

21. B
22. D
23. C
24. D
25. B

TEST 3

DIRECTIONS: Each question or incomplete statement is followed by several suggested answers or completions. Select the one that BEST answers the question or completes the statement. *PRINT THE LETTER OF THE CORRECT ANSWER IN THE SPACE AT THE RIGHT.*

1. An administrator who supervises other supervisors makes it a practice to set deadline dates for completion of assignments.
   A NATURAL consequence of setting deadline dates is that
   A. supervisors will usually wait until the deadline date before they give projects their wholehearted attention
   B. projects are completed sooner than if no deadline dates are set
   C. such dates are ignored even though they are conspicuously posted
   D. the frequency of errors sharply increases resulting in an inability to meet deadlines

   1.____

2. Assume that you are chairing a meeting of the members of your staff. You throw out a question to the group. No one answers your question immediately, so that you find yourself faced with silence.
   In the circumstances, it would probably be BEST for you to
   A. ask the member of the group who appears to be least attentive to repeat the question
   B. change the topic quickly
   C. repeat the question carefully, pronouncing each word, and if there is still no response, repeat the question an additional time
   D. wait for an answer since someone will usually say something to break the tension

   2.____

3. Assume that you are holding a meeting with the members of your staff. John, a member of the unit, keeps sidetracking the subject of the discussion by bringing up extraneous matters. You deal with the situation by saying to him after he has raised an immaterial point, *"That's an interesting point John, but can you show me how it ties in with what we're talking about?"*
   Your approach in this situation would GENERALLY be considered
   A. *bad*; you have prevented the group from discussing not only extraneous matters but pertinent material as well
   B. *bad*; you have seriously humiliated John in front of the entire group
   C. *good*; you have pointed out how the discussion is straying from the main topic
   D. *good*; you have prevented John from presenting extraneous matters at future meetings

   3.____

4. Assume that a senior supervisor is asked to supervise a group of staff personnel. The work of one of these staff men meets minimum standards of acceptability. However, this staff man constantly looks for something at which to take offense. In any conversation with either a fellow staff man or with a superior, he views the slightest criticism as a grave insult.

   4.____

In this case, the senior supervisor should
- A. advise the staff man that the next time he refuses to accept criticism, he will be severely reprimanded
- B. ask member of the group for advice on how to deal with this staff man
- C. make it a practice to speak calmly, slowly, and deliberately to this staff man and question him frequently to make sure that there is no breakdown in communications
- D. recognize that professional help may be required and that this problem may not be conducive to a solution by a supervisor

5. Assume that you discover that one of the staff in preparing certain papers has made a serious mistake which has become obvious.
In dealing with this situation, it would be BEST for you to begin by
- A. asking the employee how the mistake happened
- B. asking the employee to read through the papers to see whether he can correct the mistake
- C. pointing out to the employee that, while an occasional error is permissible, frequent errors can prove a source of embarrassment to all concerned
- D. pointing to the mistake and asking the employee whether he realizes the consequences of the mistake

6. You desire to develop teamwork among the members of your staff. You are assigned a case which will require that two of the staff work together if the papers are to be prepared in time. You decided to assign two employees, whom you know to be close friends, to work on these papers.
Your action in this regard would GENERALLY be considered
- A. *bad*; friends working together tend to do as little as they can get away with
- B. *bad*; people who are friends socially often find that the bonds of friendship disintegrate in work situations
- C. *good*; friends who are permitted to work together show their appreciation by utilizing every opportunity to reinforce the group leader's position of authority
- D. *good*; the evidence suggests that more work can be done in this way

7. You notice that all of the employees, without exception, take lunch hours which in your view are excessively long. You call each of them to your desk and point out that unless this practice is brought to a stop, appropriate action will be taken.
The way in which you handled this problem would GENERALLY be considered
- A. *proper*, primarily because a civil servant, no matter what his professional status, owes the public a full day's work for a full day's pay
- B. *proper*, primarily because employees need to have a clear picture of the rewards and penalties that go with public employment
- C. *improper*, primarily because group problems require group discussion which need not be formal in character
- D. *improper*, primarily because professional personnel resent having such matters as lunch hours brought to their attention

8. In communicating with superiors or subordinates, it is well to bear in mind a phenomenon known as the *halo effect*. An example of this *halo effect* occurs when we
    A. employ informal language in a formal setting as a means of attracting attention
    B. ignore the advice of someone we distrust without evaluating the advice
    C. ask people to speak up who have a tendency to speak softly or occasionally indistinctly
    D. react to a piece of good work by inquiring into the motivations of those who did the work

9. Which of the following dangers is MOST likely to arise when a work group becomes too tightly knit? The
    A. group may appoint an informal leader who gradually sets policies and standards for the group to the detriment of the agency
    B. group may be reluctant to accept new employees as members
    C. quantity and quality of work produced may tend to diminish sharply despite the group's best efforts
    D. group may focus too strongly on employee benefits at inappropriate times

10. The overall managerial problem has become more complex because each group of management specialists will tend to view the interests of the enterprise in terms which are compatible with the survival or the increase of its special function. That is, each group will have a trained capacity for its own function and a *trained incapacity* to see its relation to the whole.
    The *trained incapacity* to which the foregoing passage refers PROBABLY results from
    A. an imbalance in the number of specialists as compared with the number of generalists
    B. development by each specialized group of a certain dominant value or goal that shapes its entire way of doing things
    C. low morale accompanied by lackadaisical behavior by large segments of the managerial staff
    D. supervisory failure to inculcate pride in workmanship

11. Of the following, the MOST important responsibility of a supervisor in charge of a section is to
    A. establish close personal relationships with each of his subordinates in the section
    B. insure that each subordinate in the section knows the full range of his duties and responsibilities
    C. maintain friendly relations with his immediate supervisor
    D. protect his subordinates from criticism from any source

12. The BEST way to get a good work output from employees is to
    A. hold over them the threat of disciplinary action or removal
    B. maintain a steady, unrelenting pressure on them
    C. show them that you can do anything they can do faster and better
    D. win their respect and liking so they want to work for you

13. Supervisors should GENERALLY
    A. lean more toward management than toward their subordinates
    B. lean neither toward subordinates nor management
    C. lean more toward their subordinates than toward their management
    D. maintain a proper balance between management and subordinates

14. For a supervisor in charge of a section to ask occasionally the opinion of a subordinate concerning a problem is
    A. *desirable*; but it would be even better if the subordinate were consulted routinely on every problem
    B. *desirable*; subordinates may make good suggestions and will be pleased by being consulted
    C. *undesirable*; subordinates may be resentful if their advice is not followed
    D. *undesirable*; the supervisor should not attempt to shift his responsibilities to subordinates

15. The PRIMARY responsibility of a supervisor is to
    A. gain the confidence and make friends of all his subordinates
    B. get the work done properly
    C. satisfy his superior and gain his respect
    D. train the men in new methods for doing the work

16. In starting a work simplification study, the one of the following steps that should be taken FIRST is to
    A. break the work down into its elements
    B. draw up a chart of operations
    C. enlist the interest and cooperation of the personnel
    D. suggest alternative procedures

17. Of the following, the MOST important value of a manual of procedures is that it usually
    A. eliminates the need for on-the-job training
    B. decreases the span of control which can be exercised by individual supervisory personnel
    C. outlines methods of operation for ready reference
    D. provides concrete examples of work previously performed by employees

18. Reprimanding a subordinate when he has done something wrong should be done PRIMARILY in order to
    A. deter others from similar acts
    B. improve the subordinate in future performance
    C. maintain discipline
    D. uphold departmental rules

19. Most of the training of new employees in a public agency is USUALLY accomplished by
    A. formal classes
    B. general orientation
    C. internship
    D. on-the-job activities

20. You find that delivery of a certain item cannot possibly be made to a using agency by the date the using agency requested.
    Of the following, the MOST advisable course of action for you to take FIRST is to
    A. cancel the order and inform the using agency
    B. discuss the problem with the using agency
    C. notify the using agency to obtain the item through direct purchase
    D. schedule the delivery for the earliest possible date

21. Assume that one of your subordinates has gotten into the habit of regularly and routinely referring every small problem which arises in his work to you.
    In order to help him overcome this habit, it is generally MOST advisable for you to
    A. advise him that you do not have time to discuss each problem with him and that he should do whatever he wants
    B. ask your subordinate for his solution and approve any satisfactory approach that he suggests
    C. refuse to discuss such routine problems with him
    D. tell him that he should consider looking for another position if he does not feel competent to solve such routine problems

22. The BEST of the following reasons for developing understudies to supervisory staff is that this practice
    A. assures that capable staff will not leave their jobs since they are certain to be promoted
    B. helps to assure continued efficiency when persons in important positions leave their jobs
    C. improves morale by demonstrating to employees the opportunities for advancement
    D. provides an opportunity for giving on-the-job training

23. When a supervisor delegates some of his work to a subordinate, the
    A. supervisor retains final responsibility for the work
    B. supervisor should not check on the work until it has been completed
    C. subordinate assumes full responsibility for the successful completion of the work
    D. subordinate is likely to lose interest and get less satisfaction from the work

24. Sometimes it is necessary to give out written orders or to post written or typed information on a bulletin board rather than to merely give spoken orders. The supervisor must decide how he will do it.
    In which of the following situations would it be BETTER for him to give written rather than spoken orders?
    A. He is going to reassign a man from one unit to another under his supervision.
    B. His staff must be informed of a permanent change in a complicated operating procedure.

C. A man must be transferred from a clerical unit to an operating unit.
D. He must order a group of staff men to do a difficult and tedious inventory job to which most of them are likely to object.

25. Of the following symbolic patterns, which one is NOT representative of a normal direction in which formal organizational communications flow?

A. I B. II C. III D. IV

KEY (CORRECT ANSWERS)

1.	B		11.	B
2.	D		12.	D
3.	C		13.	D
4.	D		14.	B
5.	A		15.	B
6.	D		16.	C
7.	C		17.	C
8.	B		18.	B
9.	B		19.	D
10.	B		20.	B

21. B
22. B
23. A
24. B
25. B

SUPERVISION, ADMINISTRATION, MANAGEMENT AND ORGANIZATION

EXAMINATION SECTION
TEST 1

DIRECTIONS: Each question or incomplete statement is followed by several suggested answers or completions. Select the one that BEST answers the question or completes the statement. *PRINT THE LETTER OF THE CORRECT ANSWER IN THE SPACE AT THE RIGHT.*

1. One of the responsibilities of the supervisor is to provide top administration with information about clients and their problems that will help in the evaluation of existing policies and indicate the need for modifications.
   In order to fulfill this responsibility, it would be MOST essential for the supervisor to

   A. routinely forward all regularly prepared and recurrent reports from his subordinates to his immediate superior
   B. regularly review agency rules, regulations and policies to make sure that he has sufficient knowledge to make appropriate analyses
   C. note repeated instances of failure of staff to correctly administer a policy and schedule staff conferences for corrective training
   D. analyze reports on cases submitted by subordinates, in order to select relevant trend material to be forwarded to his superiors

2. You find that your division has a serious problem because of unusually long delays in filing reports and overdue approvals to private agencies under contract for services.
   The MOST appropriate step to take FIRST in this situation would be to

   A. request additional staff to work on reports and approvals
   B. order staff to work overtime until the backlog is eliminated
   C. impress staff with the importance of expeditious handling of reports and approvals
   D. analyze present procedures for handling reports and approvals

3. When a supervisor finds that he must communicate orally information that is significant enough to affect the entire staff, it would be MOST important to

   A. distribute a written summary of the information to his staff before discussing it orally
   B. tell his subordinate supervisors to discuss this information at individual conferences with their subordinates
   C. call a follow-up meeting of absentees as soon as they return
   D. restate and summarize the information in order to make sure that everyone understands its meaning and implications

4. Of the following, the BEST way for a supervisor to assist a subordinate who has unusually heavy work pressures is to

   A. point out that such pressures go with the job and must be tolerated
   B. suggest to him that the pressures probably result from poor handling of his workload
   C. help him to be selective in deciding on priorities during the period of pressure
   D. ask him to work overtime until the period of pressure is over

2 (#1)

5. Leadership is a basic responsibility of the supervisor. The one of the following which would be the LEAST appropriate way to fulfill this role is for the supervisor to

   A. help staff to work up to their capacities in every possible way
   B. encourage independent judgment and actions by staff members
   C. allow staff to participate in decisions within policy limits
   D. take over certain tasks in which he is more competent than his subordinates

5.____

6. Assume that you have assigned a very difficult administrative task to one of your best subordinate supervisors, but he is reluctant to take it on because he fears that he will fail in it. It is your judgment, however, that he is quite capable of performing this task.
The one of the following which is the MOST desirable way for you to handle this situation is to

   A. reassure him that he has enough skill to perform the task and that he will not be penalized if he fails
   B. reassign the task to another supervisor who is more achievement-oriented and more confident of his skills
   C. minimize the importance of the task so that he will feel it is safe for him to attempt it
   D. stress the importance of the task and the dependence of the other staff members on his succeeding in it

6.____

7. Assume that a member of your professional staff deliberately misinterprets a new state directive because he fears that its enforcement will have an adverse effect on clients. Although you consider him to be a good supervisor and basically agree with him, you should direct him to comply.
Of the following, the MOST desirable way for you to handle this situation would be to

   A. avoid a confrontation with him by transferring responsibility for carrying out the directive to another member of your staff
   B. explain to him that you are in a better position than he to assess the implications of the new directive
   C. discuss with him the basic reasons for his misinterpretation and explain why he must comply with the directive
   D. allow him to interpret the directive in his own way as long as he assumes full responsibility for his actions

7.____

8. Of the following, the MAIN reason it is important for an administrator in a large organization to properly coordinate the work delegated to subordinates is that such coordination

   A. makes it unnecessary to hold frequent staff meetings and conferences with key staff members
   B. reduces the necessity for regular evaluation of procedures and programs, production and performance of personnel
   C. results in greater economy and stricter accountability for the organization's resources
   D. facilitates integration of the contributions of the numerous staff members who are responsible for specific parts of the total workload

8.____

9. The one of the following which would NOT be an appropriate reason for the formulation of an entirely NEW policy is that it would

   A. serve as a positive affirmation of the agency's function and how it is to be carried out
   B. give focus and direction to the work of the staff, particularly in decision-making
   C. inform the public of the precise conditions under which services will be rendered
   D. provide procedures which constitute uniform methods of carrying out operations

10. Of the following, it is MOST difficult to formulate policy in an organization where

    A. work assignments are narrowly specialized by units
    B. staff members have varied backgrounds and a wide range of competency
    C. units implementing the same policy are in the same geographic location
    D. staff is experienced and fully trained

11. For a supervisor to feel that he is responsible for influencing the attitudes of his staff members is GENERALLY considered

    A. *undesirable;* attitudes of adults are emotional factors which usually cannot be changed
    B. *desirable;* certain attitudes can be obstructive and should be modified in order to provide effective service to clients
    C. *undesirable;* the supervisor should be nonjudgmental and accepting of widely different attitudes and social patterns of staff members
    D. *desirable;* influencing attitudes is a teaching responsibility which the supervisor shares with the training specialist

12. The one of the following which is NOT generally a function of the higher-level supervisor is

    A. projecting the budget and obtaining financial resources
    B. providing conditions conducive to optimum employee production
    C. maintaining records and reports as a basis for accountability and evaluation
    D. evaluating program achievements and personnel effectiveness in accordance with goals and standards

13. As a supervisor in a recently decentralized services center offering multiple services, you are given responsibility for an orientation program for professional staff on the recent reorganization of the Department.
    Of the following, the MOST appropriate step to take FIRST would be to

    A. organize a series of workshops for subordinate supervisors
    B. arrange a tour of the new geographic area of service
    C. review supervisors' reports, statistical data and other relevant material
    D. develop a resource manual for staff on the reorganized center

14. Experts generally agree that the content of training sessions should be closely related to workers' practice.
    Of the following, the BEST method of achieving this aim is for the training conference leader to

    A. encourage group discussion of problems that concern staff in their practice
    B. develop closer working relationships with top administration

4 (#1)

C. coordinate with central office to obtain feedback on problems that concern staff
D. observe workers in order to develop a pattern of problems for class discussion

15. The one of the following which is generally the MOST useful teaching tool for professional staff development is

   A. visual aids and tape recordings
   B. professional literature
   C. agency case material
   D. lectures by experts

15.____

16. The one of the following which is NOT a good reason for using group conferences as a method of supervision is to

   A. give workers a feeling of mutual support through sharing common problems
   B. save time by eliminating the need for individual conferences
   C. encourage discussion of certain problems that are not as likely to come up in individual conferences
   D. provide an opportunity for developing positive identification with the department and its programs

16.____

17. The supervisor, in his role as teacher, applies his teaching in line with his understanding of people and realizes that teaching is a highly individualized process, based on understanding of the worker as a person and as a learner. This statement implies, MOST NEARLY, that the supervisor must help the worker to

   A. overcome his biases
   B. develop his own ways of working
   C. gain confidence in his ability
   D. develop the will to work

17.____

18. Of the following, the circumstance under which it would be MOST appropriate to divide a training conference for professional staff into small workshops is when

   A. some of the trainees are not aware of the effect of their attitudes and behavior on others
   B. the trainees need to look at human relations problems from different perspectives
   C. the trainees are faced with several substantially different types of problems in their job assignments
   D. the trainees need to know how to function in many different capacities

18.____

19. Of the following, the MAIN reason why it is important to systemically evaluate a specific training program while it is in progress is to

   A. collect data that will serve as a valid basis for improving the agency's overall training program and maintaining control over its components
   B. insure that instruction by training specialists is conducted in a manner consistent with the planned design of the training program
   C. identify areas in which additional or remedial training for the training specialists can be planned and implemented
   D. provide data which are usable in effecting revisions of specific components of the training program

19.____

20. Staff development has been defined as an educational process which seeks to provide agency staff with knowledge about specific job responsibilities and to effect changes in staff attitudes and behavior patterns. Assume that you are assigned to define the educational objectives of a specific training program.
In accordance with the above concept, the MOST helpful formulation would be a statement of the

   A. purpose and goals of each training session
   B. generalized patterns of behavior to be developed in the trainees
   C. content material to be presented in the training sessions
   D. kind of behavior to be developed in the trainees and the situations in which this behavior will be applied

21. In teaching personnel under your supervision how to gather and analyze facts before attempting to solve a problem, the one of the following training methods which would be MOST effective is

   A. case study
   B. role playing
   C. programmed learning
   D. planned experience'

22. The importance of analyzing functions traditionally included in the position of caseworker, with a view toward identifying and separating those activities to be performed by the most highly skilled personnel, has been widely discussed.
Of the following, an IMPORTANT *secondary* gain which can result from such differential use of staff is that

   A. supporting job assignments can be given to persons unable to meet the demands of casework, to the satisfaction of all concerned
   B. documentation will be provided on workers who are not suited for all the duties now part of the caseworker's job
   C. caseworkers with a high level of competence in working with people can be rewarded through promotion or merit increases
   D. incompetent workers can be identified and categorized, as a basis for transfer or separation from the service

23. Of the following, a serious DISADVANTAGE of a performance evaluation system based on standardized evaluation factors is that such a system tends to

   A. exacerbate the anxieties of those supervisors who are apprehensive about determining what happens to another person
   B. subject the supervisor to psychological stress by emphasizing the incompatibility of his dual role as both judge and counselor
   C. create organizational conflict by encouraging personnel who wish to enhance their standing to become too aggressive in the performance of their duties
   D. lead many staff members to concentrate on measuring up in terms of the evaluation factors and to disregard other aspects of their work

24. Which of the following would contribute MOST to the achievement of conformity of staff activities and goals to the intent of agency policies and procedures?

   A. Effective communications and organizational discipline
   B. Changing nature of the underlying principles and desired purpose of the policies and procedures

C. Formulation of specific criteria for implementing the policies and procedures
D. Continuous monitoring of the essential effectiveness of agency operations

25. Job enlargement, a management device used by large organizations to counteract the adverse effects of specialization on employee performance, is LEAST likely to improve employee motivation if it is accomplished by

   A. lengthening the job cycle and adding a large number of similar tasks
   B. allowing the employee to use a greater variety of skills
   C. increasing the scope and complexity of the employee's job
   D. giving the employee more opportunities to make decisions

KEY (CORRECT ANSWERS)

1. D
2. D
3. D
4. C
5. D

6. A
7. C
8. D
9. D
10. B

11. B
12. A
13. A
14. A
15. C

16. B
17. B
18. C
19. A
20. D

21. A
22. A
23. D
24. A
25. A

TEST 2

DIRECTIONS: Each question or incomplete statement is followed by several suggested answers or completions. Select the one that BEST answers the question or completes the statement. *PRINT THE LETTER OF THE CORRECT ANSWER IN THE SPACE AT THE RIGHT.*

1. When a supervisor requires approval for case action on a higher level, the process used is known as

    A. administrative clearance
    B. going outside channels
    C. administrative consultation
    D. delegation of authority

    1.____

2. In delegating authority to his subordinates, the one of the following to which a GOOD supervisor should give PRIMARY consideration is the

    A. results expected of them
    B. amount of power to be delegated
    C. amount of responsibility to be delegated
    D. their skill in the performance of present tasks

    2.____

3. Of the following, the type of decision which could be SAFELY delegated to LOWER-LEVEL staff without undermining basic supervisory responsibility is one which

    A. involves a commitment that can be fulfilled only over a long period of time
    B. has fairly uncertain goals and premises
    C. has the possibility of modification built into it
    D. may generate considerable resistance from those affected by it

    3.____

4. Of the following, the MOST valuable contribution made by the informal organization in a large public service agency is that such an organization

    A. has goals and values which are usually consistent with and reinforce those of the formal organization
    B. is more flexible than the formal organization and more adaptable to changing conditions
    C. has a communications system which often contributes to the efficiency of the formal organization
    D. represents a sound basis on which to build the formal organizational structure

    4.____

5. Of the following, the condition under which it would be MOST useful for an agency to develop detailed procedures is when

    A. subordinate supervisory personnel need a structure to help them develop greater independence
    B. employees have little experience or knowledge of how to perform certain assigned tasks
    C. coordination of agency activities is largely dependent upon personal contact
    D. agency activities must continually adjust to changes in local circumstances

    5.____

6. Assume that a certain administrator has the management philosophy that his agency's responsibility is to routinize existing operations, meet each day's problems as they arise, and resolve problems with a minimum of residual effect upon himself or his agency. The possibility that this official would be able to administer his agency without running into serious difficulties would be MORE likely during a period of

    A. economic change
    B. social change
    C. economic crisis
    D. social and economic stability

    6.____

7. Some large organizations have adopted the practice of allowing each employee to establish his own performance goals, and then later evaluate himself in an individual conference with his immediate supervisor.
Of the following, a DRAWBACK of this approach is that the employee

   A. may set his goals too low and rate himself too highly
   B. cannot control those variables which may improve his performance
   C. has no guidelines for improving his performance
   D. usually finds it more difficult to criticize himself than to accept criticism from others

8. Decentralization of services cannot completely eliminate the requirement of central office approval for certain case actions. The MOST valid reason for complaint about this requirement is that

   A. unavoidable delay created by referral to central office may cause serious problems for the client
   B. it may lower morale of supervisors who are not given the authority to take final action on urgent cases
   C. the concept of role responsibility is minimized
   D. the objective of delegated responsibility tends to be negated

9. Which of the following would be the MOST useful administrative tool for the purpose of showing the sequence of operations and staff involved? A(n)

   A. organization chart   B. flow chart
   C. manual of operating procedures D. statistical review

10. The prevailing pattern of organization in large public agencies consists of a limited span of control and organization by function or, at lower levels, process.
Of the following, the PRINCIPAL effect which this pattern of organization has on the management of work is that it

   A. reduces the management burden in significant ways
   B. creates a time lag between the perception of a problem and action on it
   C. makes it difficult to direct and observe employee performance
   D. facilitates the development of employees with managerial ability

11. The one of the following which would be the MOST appropriate way to reduce tensions between line and staff personnel in public service agencies is to

   A. provide in-service training that will increase the sensitivity of line and staff personnel to their respective roles
   B. assign to staff personnel the role of providing assistance only when requested by line personnel
   C. separate staff from line personnel and provide staff with its own independent reward structure
   D. give line and staff personnel equal status in making decisions

12. In determining the appropriate span of control for subordinate supervisors, which of the following principles should be followed? The more

   A. complex the work, the broader the effective span of control
   B. similar the jobs being supervised, the more narrow the effective span of control

C. interdependent the jobs being supervised, the more narrow the effective span of control
D. unpredictable the work, the broader the effective span of control

13. A method sometimes used in public service agencies to improve upward communication is to require subordinate supervisory staff to submit to top management monthly narrative reports of any problems which they deem important for consideration.
Of the following, a major DISADVANTAGE of this method is that it may

    A. enable subordinate supervisors to avoid thinking about their problems by simply referring such matters to their superiors
    B. obscure important issues so that they are not given appropriate attention
    C. create a need for numerous staff conferences in order to handle all of the reported problems
    D. encourage some subordinate supervisors to focus on irrelevant matters and compete with each other in the length and content of their reports

14. The use of a committee as an approach to the problem of coordinating interdepartmental activities can present difficulties if the committee functions PRIMARILY as a(n)

    A. means of achieving personal objectives and goals
    B. instrument for coordinating activities that flow across departmental lines
    C. device for involving subordinate personnel in the decision-making process
    D. means of giving representation to competing interest groups

15. A study was recently made of the attitudes and perceptions of a sample of workers who had experienced a major organizational change and redefinition of their jobs as a result of separation of certain functions.
Questionnaires administered to these workers indicated that a disproportionate number of workers in the larger agencies were dissatisfied with the reorganization and their new assignments.
Of the following, the MOST plausible reason for this dissatisfaction is that workers in larger agencies are

    A. less likely to be known to management and to be personally disciplined if they expressed dissatisfaction with their new roles
    B. less likely to have the opportunity to participate in planning a reorganization and to be given consideration for the assignments they preferred
    C. given a shorter lead period to implement the changes and therefore had insufficient time to plan the reorganization and carry it out efficiently
    D. usually made up of more older members who have had routinized their work according to habit and find it more difficult to adjust to change

16. An article which recently appeared in a professional journal presents a proposal for participatory leadership, in which the goal of supervision would be development of subordinates' self-reliance, with the premise that each staff member is held accountable for his own performance.
The one of the following which would NOT be a desirable outcome of this type of supervision is the

    A. necessity for subordinates to critically examine their performance
    B. development by some subordinates of skills not possessed by the supervisor

C. establishment of a quality control unit for sample checking and identification of errors
D. relaxation of demands made on the supervisor

17. The "management by objectives" concept is a major development in the administration of services organizations. The purpose of this approach is to establish a system for

    A. reduction of waiting time
    B. planning and controlling work output
    C. consolidation of organizational units
    D. work measurement

18. Assume that you encounter a serious administrative problem in implementing a new program. After consulting with the members of your staff individually, you come up with several alternate solutions.
Of the following, the procedure which would be MOST appropriate for evaluating the relative merits of each solution would be to

    A. try all of them on a limited experimental basis
    B. break the problem down into its component parts and analyze the effect of each solution on each component in terms of costs and benefits
    C. break the problem down into its component parts, eliminate all intangibles, and measure the effect of the tangible aspects of each solution on each component in terms of costs and benefits
    D. bring the matter before your weekly staff conference, discuss the relative merits of each alternate solution, and then choose the one favored by the majority of the conference

19. When establishing planning objectives for a service program under your supervision, the one of the following principles which should be followed is that objectives

    A. are rarely verifiable if they are qualitative
    B. should be few in number and of equal importance
    C. should cover as many of the activities of the program as possible
    D. should be set in the light of assumptions about future funding

20. Assume that you have been assigned responsibility for coordinating various aspects of a program in a community services center. Which of the following administrative concepts would NOT be applicable to this assignment?

    A. Functional job analysis   B. Peer group supervision
    C. Differential use of staff   D. Systems design

21. Good administrative practice includes the use of outside consultants as an effective technique in achieving agency objectives. However, the one of the following which would NOT be an appropriate role for the consultant is

    A. provision of technical or professional expertise not otherwise available in the agency
    B. administrative direction of a new program activity
    C. facilitating coordination and communication among agency staff
    D. objective measurement of the effectiveness of agency services

22. Of the following, the MOST common fault of research projects attempting to measure the effectiveness of social programs has been their

    A. questionable methodology
    B. inaccurate findings
    C. unrealistic expectations
    D. lack of objectivity

23. One of the most difficult tasks of supervision in a modern public agency is teaching workers to cope with the hostile reactions of clients. In order to help the disconcerted worker analyze and understand a client's hostile behavior, the supervisor should FIRST

    A. encourage the worker to identify with the client's frustrations and deprivations
    B. give the worker a chance to express and accept his feelings about the client
    C. ask the worker to review his knowledge of the client and his circumstances
    D. explain to the worker that the client's anger is not directed at the worker personally

24. Determination of the level of participation, or how much of the public should participate in a given project, is a vital step in community organization.
    In order to make this determination, the FIRST action that should be taken is to

    A. develop the participants
    B. fix the goals of the project
    C. evaluate community interest in the project
    D. enlist the cooperation of community leaders

25. The one of the following which would be the MOST critical factor for SUCCESSFUL operation of a decentralized system of programs and services is

    A. periodic review and evaluation of services delivered at the community level
    B. transfer of decision-making authority to the community level wherever feasible
    C. participation of indigenous non-professionals in service delivery
    D. formulation of quantitative plans for dealing with community problems wherever feasible

KEY (CORRECT ANSWERS)

1.	A	11.	A
2.	A	12.	C
3.	C	13.	D
4.	C	14.	A
5.	B	15.	B
6.	D	16.	D
7.	A	17.	B
8.	A	18.	C
9.	B	19.	D
10.	B	20.	B

21. B
22. C
23. B
24. B
25. B

TEST 3

DIRECTIONS: Each question or incomplete statement is followed by several suggested answers or completions. Select the one that BEST answers the question or completes the statement. *PRINT THE LETTER OF THE CORRECT ANSWER IN THE SPACE AT THE RIGHT.*

1. Douglas McGregor's theory of human motivation classifies worker behavior into two distinct categories: Theory X and Theory Y. Theory X, the traditional view, states that the average man dislikes to work and will avoid work if he can, unless coerced. Theory Y holds essentially the opposite view. The executive can apply both of these theories to worker behavior BEST if he

    A. follows an "open-door" policy only with respect to his immediate subordinates
    B. recognizes his subordinates' mental and social needs as well as agency needs
    C. recognizes that executive responsibility is primarily limited to fulfillment of agency productivity goals
    D. directs his subordinate managers to follow a policy of close supervision

2. In interpersonal communications it is of paramount importance to determine whether or not what has been said has been understood by others. One of the MOST important sources of such information is known as

    A. the halo effect B. evaluation
    C. feedback D. quantitative analysis

3. The grapevine most often provides a USEFUL service by

    A. correcting some of the deficiencies of the formal communication system
    B. rapidly conveying a true picture of events
    C. involving staff in current organizational changes
    D. interfering with the operation of the formal communication system

4. People who are in favor of a leadership style in which the subordinates help make decisions, contend that it produces favorable effects in a work unit. According to these people, which of the following is NOT likely to be an effect of such "participative management"?

    A. Reduced turnover
    B. Accelerated learning of duties
    C. Greater acceptance of change
    D. Reduced acceptance of the work unit's goals

5. Employees of a public service agency will be MOST likely to develop meaningful goals for both the agency and the employee and become committed to attaining them if supervisors

    A. allow them unilaterally to set their own goals
    B. provide them with a clear understanding of the premises underlying the agency's goals
    C. encourage them to concentrate on setting only short-range goals for themselves
    D. periodically review the agency's goals in order to suggest changes in accordance with current conditions

6. The insights of Chester Barnard have influenced the development of management thought in significant ways. He is MOST closely identified with a position that has become known as the

   A. acceptance theory of authority
   B. principle of the manager's or executive's span of control
   C. "Theory X" and "Theory Y" dichotomy
   D. unity of command principle

7. If a manager believes that man is primarily motivated by economic incentives and, above all, seeks security, he MOST usually should operate on the assumption that his subordinates

   A. need to be closely directed and have relatively little ambition
   B. are more responsive to the social forces of their peer group than to the incentives of management
   C. are capable of learning not only to accept but to seek responsibility
   D. are capable of responding favorably to many different kinds of managerial strategies

8. Of the following, the MOST important reason why it is in the interest of public service agencies to involve subordinate personnel in setting goals is that the more committed employees are to the goals of their agency the

   A. *more* likely they are to develop a desire for the agency's achievement of success
   B. *more* likely they are to prefer difficult rather than easy tasks
   C. *more* likely they are to perceive their individual performance as a reliable indicator of the agency's performance
   D. *less* likely they are to choose unreasonably difficult goals

9. As a result of gaining more recent knowledge about motivation, modern executives have had to rethink their notions about what motivates their subordinate managers. Which of the following factors is GENERALLY considered MOST important in modern motivation theory?

   A. Fringe benefits
   B. Working conditions
   C. Recognition of good work performance
   D. Education and experience required for the job

10. Of the following, the MAIN reason why cooperative interrelationships among personnel are more likely than competitive interrelationships to promote efficiency in the operation of a public service agency is that cooperation

    A. allows for a greater degree of specialization by function
    B. increases the opportunities for employees to check on each others' work
    C. provides a feeling of identification with the organization and enhances the desire for accomplishment
    D. improves the capacity of employees to acquire knowledge and learn new skills

11. Four statements are given below. Three of them describe approaches which are desirable in developing a program of employee motivation. The one which does NOT describe such an approach is:

    A. "Establish attainable goals to give employees a sense of achievement."
    B. "Largely discount the self-interest motive because it is impractical to consider it."
    C. "Allow for the participation of persons included in the plans."
    D. "Base plans on group considerations as well as individual considerations."

12. It is GENERALLY acknowledged that certain conditions should exist to insure that a subordinate will decide to accept a communication as being authoritative. Which of the following is LEAST valid as a condition which should exist?

    A. The subordinate understands the communication
    B. At the time of the subordinate's decision, he views the communication as consistent with the organization's purpose and his personal interest
    C. At the time of the subordinate's decision, he views the communication as more consistent with his personal purpose than with the organization's interests
    D. The subordinate is mentally and physically able to comply with the communication

13. In exploring the effects that employee participation has on putting changes in work methods into effect, certain relationships have been established between participation and productivity. It has MOST generally been found that HIGHEST productivity occurs in groups that are given

    A. participation in the process of change only through representatives of their group
    B. no participation in the change process
    C. full participation in the change process
    D. intermittent participation in the process of change

14. Of the following statements, the one which represents a trend LEAST likely to occur in the area of employee-management relations is that:

    A. Employees will exert more influence on decisions affecting their interests.
    B. Technological change will have a stronger impact on organizations' human resources.
    C. Labor will judge management according to company profits.
    D. Government will play a larger role in balancing the interests of the parties in labor-management affairs.

15. Members of an organization must satisfy several fundamental psychological needs in order to be happy and productive. The broadest and MOST basic needs are

    A. achievement, recognition and acceptance
    B. competition, recognition and accomplishment
    C. salary increments and recognition
    D. acceptance of competition and economic reward

16. Morale has been defined as the capacity of a group of people to pull together steadily for a common purpose. Morale thus defined is MOST generally dependent on which one of the following conditions?

    A. Job security
    B. Group and individual self-confidence
    C. Organizational efficiency
    D. Physical health of the individuals

17. Assume that consideration is being given to forming a committee for the purpose of getting a new program under way which requires the coordination of several organizational units. Which one of the following would be a MAJOR weakness of using the "committee" approach in this situation?

    A. Its inappropriateness for decision-making
    B. The necessity to include line and staff employees
    C. The difficulty of achieving proper representation
    D. Its independence from the formal organization

18. Which of the following techniques is NOT used as an approach to encourage communication between individuals at the same level?

    A. The informal organization
    B. The chain of command
    C. Committee meetings
    D. Distribution of written reports

19. In everyday actual operations, downward communications MOST often concern

    A. specific directives about job performance
    B. information about worker performance
    C. information about the rationale of the job
    D. information to indoctrinate the organization's staff on goals to be achieved

20. Communication has been thought of for a long time as a vital process in a formal organization system. Of the following, the MOST accurate statement that can be made concerning this process is that

    A. decision-making depends on communication and organizational structure
    B. communication does not interact but is interdependent with organizational structure and decision-making
    C. effective decision-making is dependent on organizational structure but not on communication
    D. communication is dependent on the decision-making process but not on organizational structure

21. In coaching a subordinate manager in the use of the type of management in which subordinate employees participate, an executive would be MOST accurate in emphasizing that participative management

    A. uses consultative as opposed to democratic techniques
    B. uses democratic as opposed to consultative techniques
    C. requires the involvement of subordinates while reserving for the superior the right to make decisions
    D. requires involving subordinates and giving them the right to make most decisions

22. In most work situations, employees tend to form informal groups and relationships. The BEST way for a supervisor interested in high productivity to deal with such groups and relationships is to

    A. take them into account as much as possible when making work assignments and schedules
    B. ignore them, since such relationships and groups usually have no effect on work productivity

C. attempt to destroy such groups and relationships since they are usually counter-productive
D. ignore them, even though they are usually counterproductive, since nothing can be done about them

23. Assume that in an office an entirely new method has been introduced in the handling of applications for service and related information. Employees USUALLY approach such a sudden change in their work routine with an attitude of

   A. *apprehension,* chiefly because such a change makes them uncertain of their position
   B. *indifference,* chiefly because most people don't care what they are doing, as long as they are paid
   C. *approval,* chiefly because such a change provides a welcome change of pace in their work
   D. *acceptance,* mainly because most people prefer changes to the same routines

24. In what order should the following steps be taken when revising office procedure?
   I. To develop the improved method as determined by time and motion studies and effective workplace layout
   II. To find out how the task is now performed
   III. To apply the new method
   IV. To analyze the current method

   The CORRECT order is:

   A. IV, II, I, III
   B. II, I, III, IV
   C. I, II, IV, III
   D. II, IV, I, III

25. In contrast to broad spans of control, narrow spans of control are MOST likely to

   A. provide opportunity for more personal contact between superior and subordinate
   B. encourage decentralization
   C. stress individual initiative
   D. foster group or team effort

KEY (CORRECT ANSWERS)

1. B
2. C
3. A
4. D
5. B

6. A
7. A
8. A
9. C
10. C

11. B
12. C
13. C
14. C
15. A

16. B
17. A
18. B
19. A
20. A

21. C
22. A
23. A
24. D
25. A

PREPARING WRITTEN MATERIAL

PARAGRAPH REARRANGEMENT
COMMENTARY

The sentences that follow are in scrambled order. You are to rearrange them in proper order and indicate the letter choice containing the correct answer at the space at the right.

Each group of sentences in this section is actually a paragraph presented in scrambled order. Each sentence in the group has a place in that paragraph; no sentence is to be left out. You are to read each group of sentences and decide upon the best order in which to put the sentences so as to form a well-organized paragraph.

The questions in this section measure the ability to solve a problem when all the facts relevant to its solution are not given.

More specifically, certain positions of responsibility and authority require the employee to discover connection between events sometimes, apparently, unrelated. In order to do this, the employee will find it necessary to correctly infer that unspecified events have probably occurred or are likely to occur. This ability becomes especially important when action must be taken on incomplete information.

Accordingly, these questions require competitors to choose among several suggested alternatives, each of which presents a different sequential arrangement of the events. Competitors must choose the MOST logical of the suggested sequences.

In order to do so, they may be required to draw on general knowledge to infer missing concepts or events that are essential to sequencing the given events. Competitors should be careful to infer only what is essential to the sequence. The plausibility of the wrong alternatives will always require the inclusion of unlikely events or of additional chains of events which are NOT essential to sequencing the given events.

It's very important to remember that you are looking for the best of the four possible choices, and that the best choice of all may not even be one of the answers you're given to choose from.

There is no one right way to solve these problems. Many people have found it helpful to first write out the order of the sentences, as they would have arranged them, on their scrap paper before looking at the possible answers. If their optimum answer is there, this can save them some time. If it isn't, this method can still give insight into solving the problem. Others find it most helpful to just go through each of the possible choices, contrasting each as they go along. You should use whatever method feels comfortable and works for you.

While most of these types of questions are not that difficult, we've added a higher percentage of the difficult type, just to give you more practice. Usually there are only one or two questions on this section that contain such subtle distinctions that you're unable to answer confidently. And you then may find yourself stuck deciding between two possible choices, neither of which you're sure about.

EXAMINATION SECTION

TEST 1

DIRECTIONS: The following groups of sentences need to be arranged in an order that makes sense. Select the letter preceding the sequence that represents the BEST sentence order. *PRINT THE LETTER OF THE CORRECT ANSWER IN THE SPACE AT THE RIGHT.*

1.
   I. The keyboard was purposely designed to be a little awkward to slow typists down.
   II. The arrangement of letters on the keyboard of a typewriter was not designed for the convenience of the typist.
   III. Fortunately, no one is suggesting that a new keyboard be designed right away.
   IV. If one were, we would have to learn to type all over again.
   V. The reason was that the early machines were slower than the typists and would jam easily.
   The CORRECT answer is:
   A. I, III, IV, II, V
   B. II, V, I, IV, III
   C. V, I, II, III, IV
   D. II, I, V, III, IV

2.
   I. The majority of the new service jobs are part-time or low-paying.
   II. According to the U.S. Bureau of Labor Statistics, jobs in the service sector constitute 72% of all jobs in this country.
   III. If more and more workers receive less and less money, who will buy the goods and services needed to keep the economy going?
   IV. The service sector is by far the fastest growing part of the United States economy.
   V. Some economists look upon this trend with great concern.
   The CORRECT answer is:
   A. II, IV, I, V, III
   B. II, III, IV, I, V
   C. V, IV, II, III, I
   D. III, I, II, IV, V

3.
   I. They can also affect one's endurance.
   II. This can stabilize blood sugar levels, and ensure that the brain is receiving a steady, constant, supply of glucose, so that one is *hitting on all cylinders* while taking the test.
   III. By food, we mean real food, not junk food or unhealthy snacks.
   IV. For this reason, it is important not to skip a meal, and to bring food with you to the exam.
   V. One's blood sugar levels can affect how clearly one is able to think and concentrate during an exam.
   The CORRECT answer is:
   A. V, IV, II, III, I
   B. V, II, I, IV, III
   C. V, I, IV, III, II
   D. V, IV, I, III, II

1.____

2.____

3.____

4. I. Those who are the embodiment of desire are absorbed in material quests, and those who are the embodiment of feeling are warriors who value power more than possession.
    II. These qualities are in everyone, but in different degrees.
    III. But those who value understanding yearn not for goods or victory, but for knowledge.
    IV. According to Plato, human behavior flows from three main sources: desire, emotion, and knowledge.
    V. In the perfect state, the industrial forces would produce but not rule, the military would protect but not rule, and the forces of knowledge, the philosopher kings, would reign.

    The CORRECT answer is:
    A. IV, V, I, II, III
    B. V, I, II, III, IV
    C. IV, III, II, I, V
    D. IV, II, I, III, V

4._____

5. I. Of the more than 26,000 tons of garbage produced daily in New York City, 12,000 tons arrive daily at Fresh Kills.
    II. In a month, enough garbage accumulates there to fill the Empire State Building.
    III. In 1937, the Supreme Court halted the practice of dumping the trash of New York City into the sea.
    IV. Although the garbage is compacted, in a few years the mounds of garbage at Fresh Kills will be the highest points south of Maine's Mount Desert Island on the Eastern Seaboard.
    V. Instead, tugboats now pull barges of much of the trash to Staten Island and the largest landfill in the world, Fresh Kills.

    The CORRECT answer is:
    A. III, V, IV, I, II
    B. III, V, II, IV, I
    C. III, V, I, II, IV
    D. III, II, V, IV, I

5._____

6. I. Communists rank equality very high, but freedom very low.
    II. Unlike communists, conservatives place a high value on freedom and a very low value on equality.
    III. A recent study demonstrated that one way to classify people's political beliefs is to look at the importance placed on two words: freedom and equality.
    IV. Thus, by demonstrating how members of these groups feel about the two words, the study has proved to be useful for political analysts in several European countries.
    V. According to the study, socialists and liberals rank both freedom and equality very high, while fascists rate both very low.

    The CORRECT answer is:
    A. III, V, I, II, IV
    B. V, IV, III, I, II
    C. III, V, IV, II, I
    D. III, I, II, IV, V

6._____

7. I. "Can there be anything more amazing than this?"
    II. If the riddle is successfully answered, his dead brothers will be brought back to life.
    III. "Even though man sees those around him dying every day," says Dharmaraj, "he still believes and acts as if he were immortal."
    IV. "What is the cause of ceaseless wonder?" asks the Lord of the Lake.
    V. In the ancient epic, The Mahabharata, a riddle is asked of one of the Pandava brothers.
    The CORRECT answer is:
    A. V, II, I, IV, III
    B. V, IV, III, I, II
    C. V, II, IV, III, I
    D. V, II, IV, I, III

8. I. On the contrary, the two main theories—the cooperative (neoclassical) theory and the radical (labor theory)—clearly rest on very different assumptions, which have very different ethical overtones.
    II. The distribution of income is the primary factor in determining the relative levels of material well-being that different groups or individuals attain.
    III. Of all issues in economics, the distribution of income is one of the most controversial.
    IV. The neoclassical theory tends to support the existing income distribution (or minor changes), while the labor theory ends to support substantial changes in the way income is distributed.
    V. The intensity of the controversy reflects the fact that different economic theories are not purely neutral, *detached* theories with no ethical or moral implications.
    The CORRECT answer is:
    A. II, I, V, IV, III
    B. III, II, V, I, IV
    C. III, V, II, I, IV
    D. III, V, IV, I, II

9. I. The pool acts as a broker and ensures that the cheapest power gets used first.
    II. Every six seconds, the pool's computer monitors all of the generating stations in the state and decides which to ask for more power and which to cut back.
    III. The buying and selling of electrical power is handled by the New York Power Pool in Guilderland, New York.
    IV. This is to the advantage of both the buying and selling utilities.
    V. The pool began operation in 1970, and consists of the state's eight electric utilities.
    The CORRECT answer is:
    A. V, I, II, III, IV
    B. IV, II, I, III, V
    C. III, V, I, IV, II
    D. V, III, IV, II, I

10. I. Modern English is much simpler grammatically than Old English.
    II. Finnish grammar is very complicated; there are some fifteen cases, for example.
    III. Chinese, a very old language, may seem to be the exception, but it is the great number of characters/words that must be mastered that makes it so difficult to learn, not its grammar.
    IV. The newest literary language—that is, written as well as spoken—is Finish, whose literary roots go back only to about the middle of the nineteenth century.
    V. Contrary to popular belief, the longer a language is been in use the simpler its grammar—not the reverse.
    The CORRECT answer is:
    A. IV, I, II, III, V
    B. V, I, IV, II, III
    C. I, II, IV, III, V
    D. IV, II, III, I, V

KEY (CORRECT ANSWERS)

1. D
2. A
3. C
4. D
5. C
6. A
7. C
8. B
9. C
10. B

TEST 2

DIRECTIONS: This type of question tests your ability to recognize accurate paraphrasing, well-constructed paragraphs, and appropriate style and tone. It is important that the answer you select contains only the facts or concepts given in the original sentences. It is also important that you be aware of incomplete sentences, inappropriate transitions, unsupported opinions, incorrect usage, and illogical sentence order. Paragraphs that do not include all the necessary facts and concepts, that distort them, or that add new ones are not considered correct.

The format for this section may vary. Sometimes, long paragraphs are given, and emphasis is placed on style and organization. Our first five questions are of this type. Other times, the paragraphs are shorter, and there is less emphasis on style and more emphasis on accurate representation of information. Our second group of five questions are of this nature.

For each of Questions 1 through 10, select the paragraph that BEST expresses the ideas contained in the sentences above it. *PRINT THE LETTER OF THE CORRECT ANSWER IN THE SPACE AT THE RIGHT.*

1. I. Listening skills are very important for managers.
    II. Listening skills are not usually emphasized.
    III. Whenever managers are depicted in books, manuals or the media, they are always talking, never listening.
    IV. We'd like you to read the enclosed handout on listening skills and to try to consciously apply them this week.
    V. We guarantee they will improve the quality of your interactions.

    A. Unfortunately, listening skills are not usually emphasized for managers. Managers are always depicted as talking, never listening. We'd like you to read the enclosed handout on listening skills. Please try to apply these principles this week. If you do, we guarantee they will improve the quality of your interactions.
    B. The enclosed handout on listening skills will be important improving the quality of your interactions. We guarantee it. All you have to do is take sometime this week to read and to consciously try to apply the principles. Listening skills are very important for manages, but they are not usually emphasized. Whenever managers are depicted in books, manuals or the media, they are always talking, never listening.
    C. Listening well is one of the most important skills a manager can have, yet it's not usually given much attention. Think about any representation of managers in books, manuals, or in the media that you may have seen. They're always talking, never listening. We'd like you to read the enclosed handout on listening skills and consciously try to apply them the rest of the week. We guarantee you will see a difference in the quality of your interactions.

1.____

D. Effective listening, one very important tool in the effective manager's arsenal, is usually not emphasized enough. The usual depiction of managers in books, manuals or the media is one in which they are always talking, never listening. We'd like you to read the enclosed handout and consciously try to apply the information contained therein throughout the rest of the week. We feel sure that you will see a marked difference in the quality of your interactions.

2.
I. Chekhov wrote three dramatic masterpieces which share certain themes and formats: Uncle Vanya, The Cherry Orchard, and The Three Sisters.
II. They are primarily concerned with the passage of time and how this erodes human aspirations.
III. The plays are haunted by the ghosts of the wasted life.
IV. The characters are concerned with life's lesser problems; however, such as the inability to make decisions, loyalty to the wrong cause, and the inability to be clear.
V. This results in sweet, almost aching, type of a sadness referred to as Chekhovian.

   A. Chekhov wrote three dramatic masterpieces: Uncle Vanya, The Cherry Orchard, and The Three Sisters. These masterpieces share certain themes and formats: the passage of time, how time erodes human aspirations, and the ghosts of wasted life. Each masterpiece is characterized by a sweet, almost aching, type of sadness that has become known as Chekhovian. The sweetness of this sadness hinges on the fact that it is not the great tragedies of life which are destroying these characters, but their minor flaws: indecisiveness, misplaced loyalty, unclarity.
   B. The Cherry Orchard, Uncle Vanya, and The Three Sisters are three dramatic masterpieces written by Chekhov that use similar formats to explore a common theme. Each is primarily concerned with the way that passing time wears down human aspirations, and each is haunted by the ghosts of the wasted life. The characters are shown struggling futilely with the lesser problems of life: indecisiveness, loyalty to the wrong cause, and the inability to be clear. These struggles create a mood of sweet, almost aching, sadness that has become known as Chekhovian.
   C. Chekhov's dramatic masterpieces are, along with The Cherry Orchard, Uncle Vanya, and The Three Sisters. These plays share certain thematic and formal similarities. They are concerned most of all with the passage of time and the way in which time erodes human aspirations. Each play is haunted by the specter of the wasted life. Chekhov's characters are caught, however, by life's lesser snares: indecisiveness, loyalty to the wrong cause, and unclarity. The characteristic mood is a sweet, almost aching type of sadness that has come to be known as Chekhovian.
   D. A Chekhovian mood is characterized by sweet, almost aching, sadness. The term comes from three dramatic tragedies by Chekhov which revolve around the sadness of a wasted life. The three masterpieces (Uncle Vanya, The Three Sisters, and The Cherry Orchard) share the same

theme and format. The plays are concerned with how the passage of time erodes human aspirations. They are peopled with characters who are struggling with life's lesser problems. These are people who are indecisive, loyal to the wrong causes, or are unable to make themselves clear.

3.
   I. Movie previews have often helped producers decide which parts of movies they should take out or leave in.
   II. The first 1933 preview of King Kong was very helpful to the producers because many people ran screaming from the theater and would not return when four men first attacked by Kong were eaten by giant spiders.
   III. The 1950 premiere of Sunset Boulevard resulted in the filming of an entirely new beginning, and a delay of six months in the film's release.
   IV. In the original opening scene, William Holden was in a morgue talking with thirty-six other "corpses" about the ways some of them had died.
   V. When he began to tell them of his life with Gloria Swanson, the audience found this hilarious, instead of taking the scene seriously.

3._____

   A. Movie previews have often helped producers decide what parts of movies they should leave in or take out. For example, the first preview of King Kong in 1933 was very helpful. In one scene, four men were first attacked by Kong and then eaten by giant spiders. Many members of the audience ran screaming from the theater and would not return. The premiere of the 1950 film Sunset Boulevard was also very helpful. In the original opening scene, William Holden was in a morgue with thirty-six other "corpses," discussing the ways some of them had died. When he began to tell them of his life with Gloria Swanson, the audience found this hilarious. They were supposed to take the scene seriously. The result was a delay of six months in the release of the film while a new beginning was added.
   B. Movie previews have often helped producers decide whether they should change various parts of a movie. After the 1933 preview of King Kong, a scene in which four men who had been attacked by Kong were eaten by giant spiders was taken out as many people ran screaming from the theater and would not return. The 1950 premiere of Sunset Boulevard also led to some changes. In the original opening scene, William Holden was in a morgue talking with thirty-six other "corpses" about the ways some of them had died. When he began to tell them of his life with Gloria Swanson, the audience found this hilarious, instead of taking the scene seriously.
   C. What do Sunset Boulevard and King Kong have in common? Both show the value of using movie previews to test audience reaction. The first 1933 preview of King Kong showed that a scene showing four men being eaten by giant spiders after having been attacked by Kong was too frightening for many people. They ran screaming from the theater and couldn't be coaxed back. The 1950 premiere of Sunset Boulevard was also a scream, but not the kind the producers intended. The movie opens

with William Holden lying in a morgue discussing the ways they had died with thirty-six other "corpses." When he began to tell them of his life with Gloria Swanson, the audience couldn't take him seriously. Their laughter caused a six-month delay while the beginning was rewritten.

D. Producers very often use movie previews to decide if changes are needed. The premiere of Sunset Boulevard in 1950 led to a new beginning and a six-month delay in film release. At the beginning, William Holden and thirty-six other "corpses" discuss the ways some of them died. Rather than taking this seriously, the audience thought it was hilarious when he began to tell them of his life with Gloria Swanson. The first 1933 preview of King Kong was very helpful for its producers because one scene so terrified the audience that many of them ran screaming from the theater and would not return. In this particular scene, four men who had first been attacked by Kong were eaten by giant spiders.

4. I. It is common for supervisors to view employees as "things" to be manipulated. 4.____
    II. This approach does not motivate employees, nor does the carrot-and-stick approach because employees often recognize these behaviors and resent them.
    III. Supervisors can change these behaviors by using self-inquiry and persistence.
    IV. The best managers genuinely respect those they work with, are supportive and helpful, and are interested in working as a team with those they supervise.
    V. They disagree with the Golden Rule that says "he or she who has the gold makes the rules."

    A. Some managers act as if they think the Golden Rule means "he or she who has the gold makes the rules." They show disrespect to employees by seeing them as "things" to be manipulated. Obviously, this approach does not motivate employees any more than the carrot-and-stick approach motivates them. The employees are smart enough to spot these behaviors and resent them. On the other hand, the managers genuinely respect those they work with, are supportive and helpful, and are interested in working as a team. Self-inquiry and persistence can change even the former type of supervisor into the latter.
    B. Many supervisors all into the trap of viewing employees as "things" to be manipulated, or try to motivate them by using a carrot-and-stick approach. These methods do not motivate employees, who often recognize the behaviors and resent them. Supervisors can change these behaviors, however, by using self-inquiry and persistence. The best managers are supportive and helpful, and have genuine respect for those with whom they work. They are interested in working as a team with those they supervise. To them, the Golden Rule is not "he or she who has the gold makes the rules."
    C. Some supervisors see employees as "things" to be used or manipulated using a carrot-and-stick technique. These methods don't work. Employees often see through them and resent them. A supervisor who

wants to change may do so. The techniques of self-inquiry and persistence can be used to turn him or her into the type of supervisor who doesn't think the Golden Rule is "he or she who has the gold makes the rules." They may become like the best managers who treat those with whom they work with respect and give them help and support. These are the manager who know how to build a team.

   D. Unfortunately, many supervisors act as if their employees are objects whose movements they can position at will. This mistaken belief has the same result as another popular motivational technique—the carrot-and-stick approach. Both attitudes can lead to the same result—resentment from those employees who recognize the behaviors for what they are. Supervisors who recognize these behaviors can change through the use of persistence and the use of self-inquiry. It's important to remember that the best managers respect their employees. They readily give necessary help and support and are interested in working as a team with those they supervise. To these managers, the Golden Rule is not "he or she who has the gold makes the rules."

5. I. The first half of the nineteenth century produced a group of pessimistic poets—Byron, De Musset, Heine, Pushkin, and Leopardi.
   II. It also produced a group of pessimistic composers—Schubert, Chopin, Schumann, and even the later Beethoven.
   III. Above all, in philosophy, there was the profoundly pessimistic philosopher, Schopenhauer.
   IV. The Revolution was dead, the Bourbons were restored, the feudal barons were reclaiming their land, and progress everywhere was being suppressed, as the great age was over.
   V. "I thank God," said Goethe, "that I am not young in so thoroughly finished a world."

   A. "I thank God," said Goethe, "that I am not young in so thoroughly finished a world." The Revolution was dead, the Bourbons were restored, the feudal barons were reclaiming their land, and progress everywhere was being suppressed. The first half of the nineteenth century produced a group of pessimistic poets: Byron, De Musset, Heine, Pushkin, and Leopardi. It also produced pessimistic composers: Schubert, Chopin, Schumann. Although Beethoven came later, he fits into this group, too. Finally and above all, it also produced a profoundly pessimistic philosopher, Schopenhauer. The great age was over.
   B. The first half of the nineteenth century produced a group of pessimistic poets: Byron, De Musset, Heine, Pushkin, and Leopardi. It produced a group of pessimistic composers: Schubert, Chopin, Schumann, and even the later Beethoven. Above all, it produced a profoundly pessimistic philosopher, Schopenhauer. For each of these men, the great age was over. The Revolution was dead, and the Bourbons were restored. The feudal barons were reclaiming their land, and progress everywhere was being suppressed.

5.____

C. The great age was over. The Revolution was dead—the Bourbons were restored, and the feudal barons were reclaiming their land. Progress everywhere was being suppressed. Out of this climate came a profound pessimism. Poets, like Byron, De Musset, Heine, Pushkin, and Leopardi; composers, like Schubert, Chopin, Schumann, and even the later Beethoven; and above all, a profoundly pessimistic philosopher, Schopenauer. This pessimism which arose in the first half of the nineteenth century is illustrated by these words of Goethe, "I thank God that I am not young in so thoroughly finished a world."

D. The first half of the nineteenth century produced a group of pessimistic poets, Byron, De Musset, Heine, Pushkin, and Leopardi—and a group of pessimistic composers, Schubert, Chopin, Schumann, and the later Beethoven. Above it all, it produced a profoundly pessimistic philosopher, Schopenhauer. The great age was over. The Revolution was dead, the Bourbons were restored, the feudal barons were reclaiming their land, and progress everywhere was being suppressed. "I thank God," said Goethe, "that I am not young in so thoroughly finished a world."

6.
I. A new manager sometimes may feel insecure about his or her competence in the new position.
II. The new manager may then exhibit defensive or arrogant behavior towards those one supervises, or the new manager may direct overly flattering behavior toward one's new supervisor.

6._____

A. Sometimes, a new manager may feel insecure about his or her ability to perform well in this new position. The insecurity may lead him or her to treat others differently. He or she may display arrogant or defensive behavior towards those he or she supervises, or be overly flattering to his or her new supervisor.
B. A new manager may sometimes feel insecure about his or her ability to perform well in the new position. He or she may then become arrogant, defensive, or overly flattering towards those he or she works with.
C. There are times when a new manager may be insecure about how well he or she can perform in the new job. The new manager may also behave defensive or act in an arrogant way towards those he or she supervises, or overly flatter his or her boss.
D. Sometimes a new manager may feel insecure about his or her ability to perform well in the new position. He or she may then display arrogant or defensive behavior towards those they supervise, or become overly flattering towards their supervisors.

7.
I. It is possible to eliminate unwanted behavior by bringing it under stimulus control—tying the behavior to a cue, and then never, or rarely, giving the cue.
II. One trainer successfully used this method to keep an energetic young porpoise from coming out of her tank whenever she felt like it, which was potentially dangerous.
III. Her trainer taught her to do it for a reward, in response to a hand signal, and then rarely gave the signal.

7._____

A. Unwanted behavior can be eliminated by tying the behavior to a cue, and then never, or rarely, giving the cue. This is called stimulus control. One trainer was able to use this method to keep an energetic young porpoise from coming out of her tank by teaching her to come out for a reward in response to a hand signal, and then rarely giving the signal.
B. Stimulus control can be used to eliminate unwanted behavior. In this method, behavior is tied to a cue, and then the cue is rarely, if ever, given. One trainer was able to successfully use stimulus control to keep an energetic young porpoise from coming out of her tank whenever she felt like it—a potentially dangerous practice. She taught the porpoise to come out for a reward when she gave a hand signal, and then rarely gave the signal.
C. It is possible to eliminate behavior that is undesirable by bringing it under stimulus control by tying behavior to a signal, and then rarely giving the signal. One trainer successfully used this method to keep an energetic porpoise from coming out of her tank, a potentially dangerous situation. Her trainer taught the porpoise to do it for a reward, in response to a hand signal, and then would rarely give the signal.
D. By using stimulus control, it is possible to eliminate unwanted behavior by tying the behavior to a cue, and then rarely or never give the cue. One trainer was able to use this method to successfully stop a young porpoise from coming out of her tank whenever she felt like it. To curb this potentially dangerous practice, the porpoise was taught by the trainer to come out of the tank for a reward, in response to a hand signal, and then rarely given the signal.

8. I. There is a great deal of concern over the safety of commercial trucks, caused by their greatly increased role in serious accidents since federal deregulation in 1981.
   II. Recently, 60 percent of trucks in New York and Connecticut and 70 percent of trucks in Maryland randomly stopped by state troopers failed safety inspections.
   III. Sixteen states in the United States require no training at all for truck drivers.

   A. Since federal deregulation in 1981, there has been a great deal of concern over the safety of commercial trucks, and their greatly increased role in serious accidents. Recently, 60 percent of trucks in New York and Connecticut, and 70 percent of trucks in Maryland failed safety inspections. Sixteen states in the United States require no training at all for truck drivers.
   B. There is a great deal of concern over the safety of commercial trucks since federal deregulation in 1981. Their role in serious accidents has greatly increased. Recently, 60 percent of trucks randomly stopped in Connecticut and New York and 70 percent in Maryland failed safety inspections conducted by state troopers. Sixteen states in the United States provide no training at all for truck drivers.
   C. Commercial trucks have a greatly increased role in serious accidents since federal deregulation in 1981. This has led to a great deal of concern.

8.____

Recently, 70 percent of trucks in Maryland and 60 percent of trucks in New York and Connecticut failed inspection of those that were randomly stopped by state troopers. Sixteen states in the United States require no training for all truck drivers.

D. Since federal deregulation in 1981, the role that commercial trucks have played in serious accidents has greatly increased, and this has led to a great deal of concern. Recently, 60 percent of trucks in New York and Connecticut, and 70 percent of trucks in Maryland randomly stopped by state troopers failed safety inspections. Sixteen states in the U.S. don't require any training for truck drivers.

9.
I. No matter how much some people have, they still feel unsatisfied and want more, or want to keep what they have forever.
II. One recent television documentary showed several people flying from New York to Paris for a one-day shopping spree to buy platinum earrings, because they were bored.
III. In Brazil, some people were ordering coffins that cost a minimum of $45,000 and are equipping them with deluxe stereos, televisions, and other graveyard necessities.

9._____

A. Some people, despite having a great deal, still feel unsatisfied and want more, or think they can keep what they have forever. One recent documentary on television showed several people enroute from Paris to New York for a one day shopping spree to buy platinum earrings, because they were bored. Some people in Brazil are even ordering coffins equipped with such graveyard necessities as deluxe stereos and televisions. The price of the coffins start at $45,000.
B. No matter how much some people have, they may feel unsatisfied. This leads them to want more, or to want to keep what they have forever. Recently, a television documentary depicting several people flying from New York to Paris for a one day shopping spree to buy platinum earrings. They were bored. Some people in Brazil are ordering coffins that cost at least $45,000 and come equipped with deluxe televisions, stereos and other necessary graveyard items.
C. Some people will be dissatisfied no matter how much they have. They may want more, or they may want to keep what they have forever. One recent television documentary showed several people, motivated by boredom, jetting from New York to Paris for a one-day shopping spree to buy platinum earrings. In Brazil, some people are ordering coffins equipped with deluxe stereos, televisions and other graveyard necessities. The minimum price for these coffins—$45,000.
D. Some people are never satisfied. No matter how much they have they still want more, or think they can keep what they have forever. One television documentary recently showed several people flying from New York to Paris for the day to buy platinum earrings because they were bored. In Brazil, some people are ordering coffins that cost $45,000 and are equipped with deluxe stereos, televisions and other graveyard necessities.

10. I. A television signal or video signal has three parts.
    II. Its parts are the black-and-white portion, the color portion, and the synchronizing (sync) pulses, which keep the picture stable.
    III. Each video source, whether it's a camera or a video-cassette recorder contains its own generator of these synchronizing pulses to accompany the picture that it's sending in order to keep it steady and straight.
    IV. In order to produce a clean recording, a video-cassette recorder must "lock-up" to the sync pulses that are part of the video it is trying to record, and this effort may be very noticeable if the device does not have gunlock.

    10.____

    A. There are three parts to a television or video signal: the black-and-white part, the color part, and the synchronizing (sync) pulses, which keep the picture stable. Whether it's a video-cassette recorder or a camera, each video source contains its own pulse that synchronizes and generates the picture it's sending in order to keep it straight and steady. A video-cassette recorder must "lock up" to the sync pulses that are part of the video it's trying to record. If the device doesn't have gunlock, this effort must be very noticeable.
    B. A video signal or television is comprised of three parts: the black-and-white portion, the color portion, and the sync (synchronizing) pulses, which keep the picture stable. Whether it's a camera or a video-cassette recorder, each video source contains its own generator of these synchronizing pulses. These accompany the picture that it's sending in order to keep it straight and steady. A video-cassette recorder must "lock up" to the sync pulses that are part of the video it is trying to record in order to produce a clean recording. This effort may be very noticeable if the device does not have gunlock.
    C. There are three parts to a television or video signal: the color portion, the black-and-white portion, and the sync (synchronizing pulses). These keep the picture stable. Each video source, whether it's a video-cassette recorder or a camera, generates these synchronizing pulses accompanying the picture it's sending in order to keep it straight and steady. If a clean recording is to be produced, a video-cassette recorder must store the sync pulses that are part of the video it is trying to record. This effort may not be noticeable if the device does not have gunlock.
    D. A television signal or video signal has three parts: the black-and-white portion, the color portion, and the synchronizing (sync) pulses. It's the sync pulses which keep the picture stable, which accompany it and keep it steady and straight. Whether it's a camera or a video-cassette recorder, each video source contains its own generator of these synchronizing pulses. To produce a clean recording, a video-cassette recorder must "lock up" to the sync pulses that are part of the video it is trying to record. If the device does not have gunlock, this effort may be very noticeable.

KEY (CORRECT ANSWERS)

1. C
2. B
3. A
4. B
5. D
6. A
7. B
8. D
9. C
10. D

PREPARING WRITTEN MATERIAL
EXAMINATION SECTION
TEST 1

DIRECTIONS: Each question consists of a sentence which may or may not be an example of good English usage. Examine each sentence, considering grammar, punctuation, spelling, capitalization, and awkwardness. Then choose the correct statement about it from the four choices below it. If the English usage in the sentence given is better than any of the changes suggested in choices B, C, or D, pick choice A. (Do not pick a choice that will change the meaning of the sentence.) *PRINT THE LETTER OF THE CORRECT ANSWER IN THE SPACE AT THE RIGHT.*

1. We attended a staff conference on Wednesday the new safety and fire rules were discussed. 1.____
   A. This is an example of acceptable writing.
   B. The words "safety," "fire," and "rules" should begin with capital letters.
   C. There should be a comma after the word "Wednesday."
   D. There should be a period after the word "Wednesday" and the word "the" should begin with a capital letter.

2. Neither the dictionary or the telephone directory could be found in the office library. 2.____
   A. This is an example of acceptable writing.
   B. The word "or" should be changed to "nor."
   C. The word "library" should be spelled "libery."
   D. The word "neither" should be changed to "either."

3. The report would have been typed correctly if the typist could read the draft. 3.____
   A. This is an example of acceptable writing.
   B. The word "would" should be removed.
   C. The word "have" should be inserted after the word "could."
   D. The word "correctly" should be changed to "correct."

4. The supervisor brought the reports and forms to an employees desk. 4.____
   A. This is an example of acceptable writing.
   B. The word "brought" should be changed to "took."
   C. There should be a comma after the word "reports" and a comma after the word "forms."
   D. The word "employees" should be spelled "employee's."

5. It's important for all the office personnel to submit their vacation schedules on time. 5.____
   A. This is an example of acceptable writing.
   B. The word "It's" should be spelled "Its."
   C. The word "their" should be spelled "they're."
   D. The word "personnel" should be spelled "personal."

147

6. The report, along with the accompanying documents, were submitted for review.
   A. This is an example of acceptable writing.
   B. The words "were submitted" should be changed to "was submitted."
   C. The word "accompanying" should be spelled "accompaning."
   D. The comma after the word "report" should be taken out.

7. If others must use your files, be certain that they understand how the system works, but insist that you do all the filing and refiling.
   A. This is an example of acceptable writing.
   B. There should be a period after the word "works," and the word "but" should start a new sentence.
   C. The words "filing" and "refiling" should be spelled "fileing" and "refileing."
   D. There should be a comma after the word "but."

8. The appeal was not considered because of its late arrival.
   A. This is an example of acceptable writing.
   B. The word "its" should be changed to "it's."
   C. The word "its" should be changed to "the."
   D. The words "late arrival" should be changed to "arrival late."

9. The letter must be read carefuly to determine under which subject it should be filed.
   A. This is an example of acceptable writing.
   B. The word "under" should be changed to "at."
   C. The word "determine" should be spelled "determin."
   D. The word "carefuly" should be spelled "carefully."

10. He showed potential as an office manager, but he lacked skill in delegating work.
    A. This is an example of acceptable writing.
    B. The word "delegating" should be spelled "delagating."
    C. The word "potential" should be spelled "potencial."
    D. The words "he lacked" should be changed to "was lacking."

KEY (CORRECT ANSWERS)

1.	D	6.	B
2.	B	7.	A
3.	C	8.	A
4.	D	9.	D
5.	A	10.	A

TEST 2

DIRECTIONS: Each question consists of a sentence which may or may not be an example of good English usage. Examine each sentence, considering grammar, punctuation, spelling, capitalization, and awkwardness. Then choose the correct statement about it from the four choices below it. If the English usage in the sentence given is better than any of the changes suggested in choices B, C, or D, pick choice A. (Do not pick a choice that will change the meaning of the sentence.) *PRINT THE LETTER OF THE CORRECT ANSWER IN THE SPACE AT THE RIGHT.*

1. The supervisor wants that all staff members report to the office at 9:00 A.M.
   A. This is an example of acceptable writing.
   B. The word "that" should be removed and the word "to" should be inserted after the word "members."
   C. There should be a comma after the word "wants" and a comma after the word "office."
   D. The word "wants" should be changed to "want" and the word "shall" should be inserted after the word "members."

2. Every morning the clerk opens the office mail and distributes it.
   A. This is an example of acceptable writing.
   B. The word "opens" should be changed to "open."
   C. The word "mail" should be changed to "letters."
   D. The word "it" should be changed to "them."

3. The secretary typed more fast on a desktop computer than on a laptop computer.
   A. This is an example of acceptable writing.
   B. The words "more fast" should be changed to "faster."
   C. There should be a comma after the words "desktop computer."
   D. The word "than" should be changed to "then."

4. The new stenographer needed a desk a computer, a chair and a blotter.
   A. This is an example of acceptable writing.
   B. The word "blotter" should be spelled "blodder."
   C. The word "stenographer" should begin with a capital letter.
   D. There should be a comma after the word "desk."

5. The recruiting officer said, "There are many different goverment jobs available."
   A. This is an example of acceptable writing.
   B. The word "There" should not be capitalized.
   C. The word "government" should be spelled "government."
   D. The comma after the word "said" should be removed.

6. He can recommend a mechanic whose work is reliable.
   A. This is an example of acceptable writing.
   B. The word "reliable" should be spelled "relyable."
   C. The word "whose" should be spelled "who's."
   D. The word "mechanic should be spelled "mecanic."

7. She typed quickly; like someone who had not a moment to lose. 7._____
   A. This is an example of acceptable writing.
   B. The word "not" should be removed.
   C. The semicolon should be changed to a comma.
   D. The word "quickly" should be placed before instead of after the word "typed."

8. She insisted that she had to much work to do. 8._____
   A. This is an example of acceptable writing.
   B. The word "insisted" should be spelled "incisted."
   C. The word "to" used in front of "much" should be spelled "too."
   D. The word "do" should be changed to "be done."

9. He excepted praise from his supervisor for a job well done. 9._____
   A. This is an example of acceptable writing.
   B. The word "excepted" should be spelled "accepted."
   C. The order of the words "well done" should be changed to "done well."
   D. There should be a comma after the word "supervisor."

10. What appears to be intentional errors in grammar occur several times in the passage. 10._____
    A. This is an example of acceptable writing.
    B. The word "occur" should be spelled "occurr."
    C. The word "appears" should be changed to "appear."
    D. The phrase "several times" should be changed to "from time to time."

KEY (CORRECT ANSWERS)

1. B   6. A
2. A   7. C
3. B   8. C
4. D   9. B
5. C   10. C

TEST 3

DIRECTIONS: Each question consists of a sentence which may or may not be an example of good English usage. Examine each sentence, considering grammar, punctuation, spelling, capitalization, and awkwardness. Then choose the correct statement about it from the four choices below it. If the English usage in the sentence given is better than any of the changes suggested in choices B, C, or D, pick choice A. (Do not pick a choice that will change the meaning of the sentence.) *PRINT THE LETTER OF THE CORRECT ANSWER IN THE SPACE AT THE RIGHT.*

1. The clerk could have completed the assignment on time if he knows where these materials were located.
    A. This is an example of acceptable writing.
    B. The word "knows" should be replaced by "had known."
    C. The word "were" should be replaced by "had been."
    D. The words "where these materials were located" should be replaced by "the location of these materials."

1.____

2. All employees should be given safety training. Not just those who accidents.
    A. This is an example of acceptable writing.
    B. The period after the word "training" should be changed to a colon.
    C. The period after the word "training" should be changed to a semicolon, and the first letter of the word "Not" should be changed to a small "n."
    D. The period after the word "training" should be changed to a comma, and the first letter of the word "Not" should be changed to a small "n."

2.____

3. This proposal is designed to promote employee awareness of the suggestion program, to encourage employee participation in the program, and to increase the number of suggestions submitted.
    A. This is an example of acceptable writing.
    B. The word "proposal" should be spelled "proposal."
    C. The words "to increase the number of suggestions submitted" should be changed to "an increase in the number of suggestions is expected."
    D. The word "promote" should be changed to "enhance" and the word "increase" should be changed to "add to."

3.____

4. The introduction of inovative managerial techniques should be preceded by careful analysis of the specific circumstances and conditions in each department.
    A. This is an example of acceptable writing.
    B. The word "technique" should be spelled "techneques."
    C. The word "inovative" should be spelled "innovative."
    D. A comma should be placed after the word "circumstances" and after the word "conditions."

4.____

5. This occurrence indicates that such criticism embarrasses him. 5.____
   A. This is an example of acceptable writing.
   B. The word "occurrence" should be spelled "occurence."
   C. The word "criticism" should be spelled "critisism.
   D. The word "embarrasses" should be spelled "embarasses.

KEY (CORRECT ANSWERS)

1. B
2. D
3. A
4. C
5. A

RECORD KEEPING
EXAMINATION SECTION
TEST 1

DIRECTIONS: Each question or incomplete statement is followed by several suggested answers or completions. Select the one that BEST answers the question or completes the statement. *PRINT THE LETTER OF THE CORRECT ANSWER IN THE SPACE AT THE RIGHT.*

Questions 1-7.

DIRECTIONS: In answering Questions 1 through 7, use the following master list. For each question, determine where the name would fit on the master list. Each answer choice indicates right before or after the name in the answer choice.

        Aaron, Jane
        Armstead, Brendan
        Bailey, Charles
        Dent, Ricardo
        Grant, Mark
        Mars, Justin
        Methieu, Justine
        Parker, Cathy
        Sampson, Suzy
        Thomas, Heather

1. Schmidt, William
   A. Right before Cathy Parker
   B. Right after Heather Thomas
   C. Right after Suzy Sampson
   D. Right before Ricardo Dent

2. Asanti, Kendall
   A. Right before Jane Aaron
   B. Right after Charles Bailey
   C. Right before Justine Methieu
   D. Right after Brendan Armstead

3. O'Brien, Daniel
   A. Right after Justine Methieu
   B. Right before Jane Aaron
   C. Right after Mark Grant
   D. Right before Suzy Sampson

4. Marrow, Alison
   A. Right before Cathy Parker
   B. Right before Justin Mars
   C. Right before Mark Grant
   D. Right after Heather Thomas

5. Grantt, Marissa
   A. Right before Mark Grant
   B. Right after Mark Grant
   C. Right after Justin Mars
   D. Right before Suzy Sampson

1.____
2.____
3.____
4.____
5.____

6. Thompson, Heath   6.____
   A. Right after Justin Mars   B. Right before Suzy Sampson
   C. Right after Heather Thomas   D. Right before Cathy Parker

DIRECTIONS: Before answering Question 7, add in all of the names from Questions 1 through 6. Then fit the name in alphabetical order based on the new list.

7. Francisco, Mildred   7.____
   A. Right before Mark Grant   B. Right after Marissa Grantt
   C. Right before Alison Marrow   D. Right after Kendall Asanti

Questions 8-10.

DIRECTIONS: In answering Questions 8 through 10, compare each pair of names and addresses. Indicate whether they are the same or different in any way.

8. William H. Pratt, J.D.   William H. Pratt, J.D.   8.____
   Attourney at Law   Attorney at Law
   A. No differences   B. 1 difference
   C. 2 differences   D. 3 differences

9. 1303 Theater Drive,; Apt. 3-B   1330 Theatre Drive,; Apt. 3-B   9.____
   A. No differences   B. 1 difference
   C. 2 differences   D. 3 differences

10. Petersdorff, Briana and Mary   Petersdorff, Briana and Mary   10.____
    A. No differences   B. 1 difference
    C. 2 differences   D. 3 differences

11. Which of the following words, if any, are misspelled?   11.____
    A. Affordable   B. Circumstansial
    C. Legalese   D. None of the above

Questions 12-13.

DIRECTIONS: Questions 12 and 13 are to be answered on the basis of the following table.

Standardized Test Results for High School Students in District #1230

	English	Math	Science	Reading
High School 1	21	22	15	18
High School 2	12	16	13	15
High School 3	16	18	21	17
High School 4	19	14	15	16

The scores for each high school in the district were averaged out and listed for each subject tested. Scores of 0-10 are significantly below College Readiness Standards. 11-15 are below College Readiness, 16-20 meet College Readiness, and 21-25 are above College Readiness.

12. If the high schools need to meet or exceed in at least half the categories in order to NOT be considered "at risk," which schools are considered "at risk"? 12.____
    A. High School 2   B. High School 3
    C. High School 4   D. Both A and C

13. What percentage of subjects did the district as a whole meet or exceed College Readiness standards? 13.____
    A. 25%   B. 50%   C. 75%   D. 100%

Questions 14-15.

DIRECTIONS: Questions 14 and 15 are to be answered on the basis of the following information.

You have seven employees working as a part of your team: Austin, Emily, Jeremy, Christina, Martin, Harriet, and Steve. You have just sent an e-mail informing them that there will be a mandatory training session next week. To ensure that work still gets done, you are offering the training twice during the week: once on Tuesday and also on Thursday. This way half the employees will still be working while the other half attend the training. The only other issue is that Jeremy doesn't work on Tuesdays and Harriet doesn't work on Thursdays due to compressed work schedules.

14. Which of the following is a possible attendance roster for the first training session? 14.____
    A. Emily, Jeremy, Steve   B. Steve, Christina, Harriet
    C. Harriet, Jeremy, Austin   D. Steve, Martin, Jeremy

15. If Harriet, Christina, and Steve attend the training session on Tuesday, which of the following is a possible roster for Thursday's training session? 15.____
    A. Jeremy, Emily, and Austin   B. Emily, Martin, and Harriet
    C. Austin, Christina, and Emily D. Jeremy, Emily, and Steve

Questions 16-20.

DIRECTIONS: In answering Questions 16 through 20, you will be given a word and will need to choose the answer choice that is MOST similar or different to the word.

16. Which word means the SAME as *annual*? 16.____
    A. Monthly   B. Usually   C. Yearly   D. Constantly

17. Which word means the SAME as *effort*? 17.____
    A. Energy   B. Equate   C. Cherish   D. Commence

18. Which word means the OPPOSITE of *forlorn*? 18.____
    A. Neglected   B. Lethargy   C. Optimistic D. Astonished

19. Which word means the SAME as *risk*? 19.____
    A. Admire   B. Hazard   C. Limit   D. Hesitant

20. Which word means the OPPOSITE of *translucent*? 20._____
    A. Opaque   B. Transparent   C. Luminous   D. Introverted

21. Last year, Jamie's annual salary was $50,000. Her boss called her today 21._____
    to inform her that she would receive a 20% raise for the upcoming year. How
    much more money will Jamie receive next year?
    A. $60,000   B. $10,000   C. $1,000   D. $51,000

22. You and a co-worker work for a temp hiring agency as part of their office 22._____
    staff. You both are given 6 days off per month. How many days off are you
    and your co-worker given in a year?
    A. 24   B. 72   C. 144   D. 48

23. If Margot makes $34,000 per year and she works 40 hours per week for 23._____
    all 52 weeks, what is her hourly rate?
    A. $16.34/hour   B. $17.00/hour   C. $15.54/hour   D. $13.23/hour

24. How many dimes are there in $175.00? 24._____
    A. 175   B. 1,750   C. 3,500   D. 17,500

25. If Janey is three times as old as Emily, and Emily is 3, how old is Janey? 25._____
    A. 6   B. 9   C. 12   D. 15

KEY (CORRECT ANSWERS)

1.	C		11.	B
2.	D		12.	A
3.	A		13.	D
4.	B		14.	B
5.	B		15.	A
6.	C		16.	C
7.	A		17.	A
8.	B		18.	C
9.	C		19.	B
10.	A		20.	A

21. B
22. C
23. A
24. B
25. B

TEST 2

DIRECTIONS: Each question or incomplete statement is followed by several suggested answers or completions. Select the one that BEST answers the question or completes the statement. *PRINT THE LETTER OF THE CORRECT ANSWER IN THE SPACE AT THE RIGHT.*

Questions 1-6.

DIRECTIONS: Questions 1 through 6 are to be answered on the basis of the following information.

item	name of item to be ordered
quantity	minimum number that can be ordered
beginning amount	amount in stock at start of month
amount received	amount receiving during month
ending amount	amount in stock at end of month
amount used	amount used during month
amount to order	will need at least as much of each item as used in the previous month
unit price	cost of each unit of an item
total price	total price for the order

Item	Quantity	Beginning	Received	Ending	Amount Used	Amount to Order	Unit Price	Total Price
Pens	10	22	10	8	24	20	$0.11	$2.20
Spiral notebooks	8	30	13	12			$0.25	
Binder clips	2 boxes	3 boxes	1 box	1 box			$1.79	
Sticky notes	3 packs	12 packs	4 packs	2 packs			$1.29	
Dry erase markers	1 pack (dozen)	34 markers	8 markers	40 markers			$16.49	
Ink cartridges (printer)	1 cartridge	3 cartridges	1 cartridge	2 cartridges			$79.99	
Folders	10 folders	25 folders	15 folders	10 folders			$1.08	

1. How many packs of sticky notes were used during the month?
   A. 16   B. 10   C. 12   D. 14

2. How many folders need to be ordered for next month?
   A. 15   B. 20   C. 30   D. 40

3. What is the total price of notebooks that you will need to order?
   A. $6.00   B. $0.25   C. $4.50   D. $2.75

4. Which of the following will you spend the second most money on?
   A. Ink cartridges   B. Dry erase markers
   C. Sticky notes   D. Binder clips

5. How many packs of dry erase markers should you order?
   A. 1   B. 8   C. 12   D. 0

6. What will be the total price of the file folders you order? 6._____
   A. $20.16   B. $21.60   C. $10.80   D. $4.32

Questions 7-11.

DIRECTIONS: Questions 7 through 11 are to be answered on the basis of the following table.

Number of Car Accidents, By Location and Cause, for 2014						
	Location 1		Location 2		Location 3	
Cause	Number	Percent	Number	Percent	Number	Percent
Severe Weather	10		25		30	
Excessive Speeding	20	40	5		10	
Impaired Driving	15		15	25	8	
Miscellaneous	5		15		2	4
TOTALS	50	100	60	100	50	100

7. Which of the following is the third highest cause of accidents for all three locations? 7._____
   A. Severe Weather
   B. Impaired Driving
   C. Miscellaneous
   D. Excessive Speeding

8. The average number of Severe Weather accidents per week at Location 3 for the year (52 weeks) was MOST NEARLY 8._____
   A. 0.57   B. 30   C. 1   D. 1.25

9. Which location had the LARGEST percentage of accidents caused by Impaired Driving? 9._____
   A. 1   B. 2   C. 3   D. Both A and B

10. If one-third of the accidents at all three locations resulted in at least one fatality, what is the LEAST amount of deaths caused by accidents last year? 10._____
    A. 60   B. 106   C. 66   D. 53

11. What is the percentage of accidents caused by miscellaneous means from all three locations in 2014? 11._____
    A. 5%   B. 10%   C. 13%   D. 25%

12. How many pairs of the following groups of letters are exactly alike? 12._____
    ACDOBJ   ACDBOJ
    HEWBWR   HEWRWB
    DEERVS   DEERVS
    BRFQSX   BRFQSX
    WEYRVB   WEYRVB
    SPQRZA   SQRPZA

    A. 2   B. 3   C. 4   D. 5

Questions 13-19.

DIRECTIONS: Questions 13 through 19 are to be answered on the basis of the following information.

In 2012, the most current information on the American population was finished. The information was compiled by 200 volunteers in each of the 50 states. The territory of Puerto Rico, a sovereign of the United States, had 25 people assigned to compile data. In February of 2010, volunteers in each state and sovereign began collecting information. In Puerto Rico, data collection finished by January 31st, 2011, while work in the United States was completed on June 30, 2012. Each volunteer gathered data on the population of their state or sovereign. When the information was compiled, volunteers sent reports to the nation's capital, Washington, D.C. Each volunteer worked 20 hours per month and put together 10 reports per month. After the data was compiled in total, 50 people reviewed the data and worked from January 2012 to December 2012.

13. How many reports were generated from February 2010 to April 2010 in Illinois and Ohio?
    A. 3,000   B. 6,000   C. 12,000   D. 15,000

14. How many volunteers in total collected population data in January 2012?
    A. 10,000   B. 2,000   C. 225   D. 200

15. How many reports were put together in May 2012?
    A. 2,000   B. 50,000   C. 100,000   D. 100,250

16. How many hours did the Puerto Rican volunteers work in the fall (September-November)?
    A. 60   B. 500   C. 1,500   D. 0

17. How many workers were compiling or reviewing data in July 2012?
    A. 25   B. 50   C. 200   D. 250

18. What was the total amount of hours worked by Nevada volunteers in July 2010?
    A. 500   B. 4,000   C. 4,500   D. 5,000

19. How many reviewers worked in January 2013?
    A. 75   B. 50   C. 0   D. 25

20. John has to file 10 documents per shelf. How many documents would it take for John to fill 40 shelves?
    A. 40   B. 400   C. 4,500   D. 5,000

21. Jill wants to travel from New York City to Los Angeles by bike, which is approximately 2,772 miles. How many miles per day would Jill need to average if she wanted to complete the trip in 4 weeks?
    A. 100   B. 89   C. 99   D. 94

22. If there are 24 CPU's and only 7 monitors, how many more monitors do you need to have the same amount of monitors as CPU's?
    A. Not enough information
    B. 17
    C. 31
    D. 0

23. If Gerry works 5 days a week and 8 hours each day, and John works 3 days a week and 10 hours each day, how many more hours per year will Gerry work than John?
    A. They work the same amount of hours.
    B. 450
    C. 520
    D. 832

24. Jimmy gets transferred to a new office. The new office has 25 employees, but only 16 are there due to a blizzard. How many coworkers was Jimmy able to meet on his first day?
    A. 16
    B. 25
    C. 9
    D. 7

25. If you do a fundraiser for charities in your area and raise $500 total, how much would you give to each charity if you were donating equal amounts to 3 of them?
    A. $250.00
    B. $167.77
    C. $50.00
    D. $111.11

KEY (CORRECT ANSWERS)

1.	D		11.	C
2.	B		12.	B
3.	A		13.	C
4.	C		14.	A
5.	D		15.	C
6.	B		16.	C
7.	D		17.	B
8.	A		18.	B
9.	A		19.	C
10.	D		20.	B

21. C
22. B
23. C
24. A
25. B

TEST 3

DIRECTIONS: Each question or incomplete statement is followed by several suggested answers or completions. Select the one that BEST answers the question or completes the statement. *PRINT THE LETTER OF THE CORRECT ANSWER IN THE SPACE AT THE RIGHT.*

Questions 1-3.

DIRECTIONS: In answering Questions 1 through 3, choose the correctly spelled word.

1. A. allusion B. alusion C. allusien D. allution 1.____

2. A. altitude B. alltitude C. atlitude D. altlitude 2.____

3. A. althogh B. allthough C. althrough D. although 3.____

Questions 4-9.

DIRECTIONS: In answering Questions 4 through 9, choose the answer that BEST completes the analogy.

4. Odometer is to mileage as compass is to 4.____
   A. speed B. needle C. hiking D. direction

5. Marathon is to race as hibernation is to 5.____
   A. winter B. dream C. sleep D. bear

6. Cup is to coffee as bowl is to 6.____
   A. dish B. spoon C. food D. soup

7. Flow is to river as stagnant is to 7.____
   A. pool B. rain C. stream D. canal

8. Paw is to cat as hoof is to 8.____
   A. lamb B. horse C. lion D. elephant

9. Architect is to building as sculptor is to 9.____
   A. museum B. chisel C. stone D. statue

Questions 10-14.

DIRECTIONS: Questions 10 through 14 are to be answered on the basis of the following graph.

Population of Carroll City Broken Down by Age and Gender (in Thousands)			
Age	Female	Male	Total
Under 15	60	60	120
15-23		22	
24-33		20	44
34-43	13	18	31
44-53	20		67
64 and Over	65	65	130
TOTAL	230	232	462

10. How many people in the city are between the ages of 15-23?
    A. 70 B. 46,000 C. 70,000 D. 225,000

11. Approximately what percentage of the total population of the city was female aged 24-33?
    A. 10% B. 5% C. 15% D. 25%

12. If 33% of the males have a job and 55% of females don't have a job, which of the following statements is TRUE?
    A. Males have approximately 2,600 more jobs than females.
    B. Females have approximately 49,000 more jobs than males.
    C. Females have approximately 26,000 more jobs than males.
    D. None of the above statements are true.

13. How many females between the ages of 15-23 live in Carroll City?
    A. 67,000 B. 24,000 C. 48,000 D. 91,000

14. Assume all males 44-53 living in Carroll City are employed. If two-thirds of males age 44-53 work jobs outside of Carroll City, how many work within city limits?
    A. 31,333
    B. 15,667
    C. 47,000
    D. Cannot answer the question with the information provided

Questions 15-16.

DIRECTIONS: Questions 15 and 16 are labeled as shown. Alphabetize them for filing. Choose the answer that correctly shows the order.

15. (1) AED
    (2) OOS
    (3) FOA
    (4) DOM
    (5) COB

    A. 2-5-4-3-2   B. 1-4-5-2-3   C. 1-5-4-2-3   D. 1-5-4-3-2

15.____

16. Alphabetize the names of the people. Last names are given last.
    (1) Lindsey Jamestown
    (2) Jane Alberta
    (3) Ally Jamestown
    (4) Allison Johnston
    (5) Lyle Moreno

    A. 2-1-3-4-5   B. 3-4-2-1-5   C. 2-3-1-4-5   D. 4-3-2-1-5

16.____

17. Which of the following words is misspelled?
    A. disgust   B. whisper
    C. locale   D. none of the above

17.____

Questions 18-21.

DIRECTIONS: Questions 18 through 21 are to be answered on the basis of the following list of employees.

    Robertson, Aaron
    Bacon, Gina
    Jerimiah, Trace
    Gillette, Stanley
    Jacks, Sharon

18. Which employee name would come in third in alphabetized list?
    A. Robertson, Aaron   B. Jerimiah, Trace
    C. Gillette, Stanley   D. Jacks, Sharon

18.____

19. Which employee's first name starts with the letter in the alphabet that is five letters after the first letter of their last name?
    A. Jerimiah, Trace   B. Bacon, Gina
    C. Jacks, Sharon   D. Gillette, Stanley

19.____

20. How many employees have last names that are exactly five letters long?
    A. 1   B. 2   C. 3   D. 4

20.____

21. How many of the employees have either a first or last name that starts with the letter "G"?
    A. 1   B. 2   C. 4   D. 5

21.____

Questions 22-25.

DIRECTIONS: Questions 22 through 25 are to be answered on the basis of the following chart.

Bicycle Sales (Model #34JA32)							
Country	May	June	July	August	September	October	Total
Germany	34	47	45	54	56	60	296
Britain	40	44	36	47	47	46	260
Ireland	37	32	32	32	34	33	200
Portugal	14	14	14	16	17	14	89
Italy	29	29	28	31	29	31	177
Belgium	22	24	24	26	25	23	144
Total	176	198	179	206	208	207	1166

22. What percentage of the overall total was sold to the German importer?
    A. 25.3%   B. 22%   C. 24.1%   D. 23%

22.____

23. What percentage of the overall total was sold in September?
    A. 24.1%   B. 25.6%   C. 17.9%   D. 24.6%

23.____

24. What is the average number of units per month imported into Belgium over the first four months shown?
    A. 26   B. 20   C. 24   D. 31

24.____

25. If you look at the three smallest importers, what is their total import percentage?
    A. 35.1%   B. 37.1%   C. 40%   D. 28%

25.____

KEY (CORRECT ANSWERS)

1. A
2. A
3. D
4. D
5. C

6. D
7. A
8. B
9. D
10. C

11. B
12. C
13. C
14. B
15. D

16. C
17. D
18. D
19. B
20. B

21. B
22. A
23. C
24. C
25. A

TEST 4

DIRECTIONS: Each question or incomplete statement is followed by several suggested answers or completions. Select the one that BEST answers the question or completes the statement. *PRINT THE LETTER OF THE CORRECT ANSWER IN THE SPACE AT THE RIGHT.*

Questions 1-6.

DIRECTIONS: In answering Questions 1 through 6, choose the sentence that represents the BEST example of English grammar.

1. A. Joey and me want to go on a vacation next week.
    B. Gary told Jim he would need to take some time off.
    C. If turning six years old, Jim's uncle would teach Spanish to him.
    D. Fax a copy of your resume to Ms. Perez and me.

    1.____

2. A. Jerry stood in line for almost two hours.
    B. The reaction to my engagement was less exciting than I thought it would be.
    C. Carlos and me have done great work on this project.
    D. Two parts of the speech needs to be revised before tomorrow.

    2.____

3. A. Arriving home, the alarm was tripped.
    B. Jonny is regarded as a stand up guy, a responsible parent, and he doesn't give up until a task is finished.
    C. Each employee must submit a drug test each month.
    D. One of the documents was incinerated in the explosion.

    3.____

4. A. As soon as my parents get home, I told them I finished all of my chores.
    B. I asked my teacher to send me my missing work, check my absences, and how did I do on my test.
    C. Matt attempted to keep it concealed from Jenny and me.
    D. If Mary or him cannot get work done on time, I will have to split them up.

    4.____

5. A. Driving to work, the traffic report warned him of an accident on Highway 47.
    B. Jimmy has performed well this season.
    C. Since finishing her degree, several job offers have been given to Cam.
    D. Our boss is creating unstable conditions for we employees.

    5.____

6. A. The thief was described as a tall man with a wiry mustache weighing approximately 150 pounds.
    B. She gave Patrick and I some more time to finish our work.
    C. One of the books that he ordered was damaged in shipping.
    D. While talking on the rotary phone, the car Jim was driving skidded off the road.

    6.____

2 (#4)

Questions 7-9.

DIRECTIONS: Questions 7 through 9 are to be answered on the basis of the following graph.

Ice Lake Frozen Flight (2002-2013)		
Year	Number of Participants	Temperature (Fahrenheit)
2002	22	4°
2003	50	33°
2004	69	18°
2005	104	22°
2006	108	24°
2007	288	33°
2008	173	9°
2009	598	39°
2010	698	26°
2011	696	30°
2012	777	28°
2013	578	32°

7. Which two year span had the LARGEST difference between temperatures? 7.____
   A. 2002 and 2003   B. 2011 and 2012
   C. 2008 and 2009   D. 2003 and 2004

8. How many total people participated in the years after the temperature reached at least 29°? 8.____
   A. 2,295   B. 1,717   C. 2,210   D. 4,543

9. In 2007, the event saw 288 participants, while in 2008 that number dropped to 173. Which of the following reasons BEST explains the drop in participants? 9.____
   A. The event had not been going on that long and people didn't know about it.
   B. The lake water wasn't cold enough to have people jump in.
   C. The temperature was too cold for many people who would have normally participated.
   D. None of the above reasons explain the drop in participants.

10. In the following list of numbers, how many times does 4 come just after 2 when 2 comes just after an odd number? 10.____
    2365247653898632488572486392424
    A. 2   B. 3   C. 4   D. 5

11. Which choice below lists the letter that is as far after B as S is after N in the alphabet? 11.____
    A. G   B. H   C. I   D. J

Questions 12-15.

DIRECTIONS: Questions 12 through 15 are to be answered on the basis of the following directory and list of changes.

Directory		
Name	Emp. Type	Position
Julie Taylor	Warehouse	Packer
James King	Office	Administrative Assistant
John Williams	Office	Salesperson
Ray Moore	Warehouse	Maintenance
Kathleen Byrne	Warehouse	Supervisor
Amy Jones	Office	Salesperson
Paul Jonas	Office	Salesperson
Lisa Wong	Warehouse	Loader
Eugene Lee	Office	Accountant
Bruce Lavine	Office	Manager
Adam Gates	Warehouse	Packer
Will Suter	Warehouse	Packer
Gary Lorper	Office	Accountant
Jon Adams	Office	Salesperson
Susannah Harper	Office	Salesperson

Directory Updates:
- Employee e-mail addresses will adhere to the following guidelines: lastnamefirstname@apexindustries.com (ex. Susannah Harper is harpersusannah@apexindustries.com). Currently, employees in the warehouse share one e-mail, distribution@apexindustries.com.
- The "Loader" position will now be referred to as "Specialist I"
- Adam Gates has accepted a Supervisor position within the Warehouse and is no longer a Packer. All warehouse employees report to the two Supervisors and all office employees report to the Manager.

12. Amy Jones tried to send an e-mail to Adam Gates, but it wouldn't send. 12.____
    Which of the following offers the BEST explanation?
    A. Amy put Adam's first name first and then his last name.
    B. Adam doesn't check his e-mail, so he wouldn't know if he received the e-mail or not.
    C. Adam does not have his own e-mail.
    D. Office employees are not allowed to send e-mails to each other.

13. How many Packers currently work for Apex Industries? 13.____
    A. 2   B. 3   C. 4   D. 5

14. What position does Lisa Wong currently hold? 14.____
    A. Specialist I   B. Secretary
    C. Administrative Assistant D. Loader

15. If an employee wanted to contact the office manager, which of the following e-mails should the e-mail be sent to?   15.____
    A. officemanager@apexindustries.com
    B. brucelavine@apexindustries.com
    C. lavinebruce@apexindustries.com
    D. distribution@apexindustries.com

Questions 16-19.

DIRECTIONS: In answering Questions 16 through 19, compare the three names, numbers or addresses.

16. Smiley Yarnell   Smiley Yarnel   Smily Yarnell   16.____
    A. All three are exactly alike.
    B. The first and second are exactly alike.
    C. The second and third are exactly alike.
    D. All three are different.

17. 1583 Theater Drive   1583 Theater Drive   1583 Theatre Drive   17.____
    A. All three are exactly alike.
    B. The first and second are exactly alike.
    C. The second and third are exactly alike.
    D. All three are different.

18. 3341893212   3341893212   3341893212   18.____
    A. All three are exactly alike.
    B. The first and second are exactly alike.
    C. The second and third are exactly alike.
    D. All three are different.

19. Douglass Watkins   Douglas Watkins   Douglass Watkins   19.____
    A. All three are exactly alike.
    B. The first and third are exactly alike.
    C. The second and third are exactly alike.
    D. All three are different.

Questions 20-24.

DIRECTIONS: In answering Questions 20 through 24, you will be presented with a word. Choose the synonym that BEST represents the word in question.

20. Flexible   20.____
    A. delicate   B. inflammable   C. strong   D. pliable

21. Alternative   21.____
    A. choice   B. moderate   C. lazy   D. value

22. Corroborate
    A. examine   B. explain   C. verify   D. explain

23. Respiration
    A. recovery   B. breathing   C. sweating   D. selfish

24. Negligent
    A. lazy   B. moderate   C. hopeless   D. lax

25. Plumber is to Wrench as Painter is to
    A. pipe   B. shop   C. hammer   D. brush

22.____
23.____
24.____
25.____

KEY (CORRECT ANSWERS)

1. D
2. A
3. D
4. C
5. B

6. C
7. C
8. B
9. C
10. C

11. A
12. C
13. A
14. A
15. C

16. D
17. B
18. A
19. B
20. D

21. A
22. C
23. B
24. D
25. D

PHILOSOPHY, PRINCIPLES, PRACTICES, AND TECHNICS OF SUPERVISION, ADMINISTRATION, MANAGEMENT, AND ORGANIZATION

TABLE OF CONTENTS

	Page
MEANING OF SUPERVISION	1
THE OLD AND THE NEW SUPERVISION	1
THE EIGHT (8) BASIC PRINCIPLES OF THE NEW SUPERVISION	1
I. Principle of Responsibility	1
II. Principle of Authority	2
III. Principle of Self-Growth	2
IV. Principle of Individual Worth	2
V. Principle of Creative Leadership	2
VI. Principle of Success and Failure	2
VII. Principle of Science	3
VIII. Principle of Cooperation	3
WHAT IS ADMINISTRATION?	3
I. Practices Commonly Classed as "Supervisory"	3
II. Practices Commonly Classed as "Administrative"	3
III. Practices Commonly Classed as Both "Supervisory" and "Administrative"	4
RESPONSIBILITIES OF THE SUPERVISOR	4
COMPETENCIES OF THE SUPERVISOR	4
THE PROFESSIONAL SUPERVISOR-EMPLOYEE RELATIONSHIP	4
MINI-TEXT IN SUPERVISION, ADMINISTRATION, MANAGEMENT, AND ORGANIZATION	5
I. Brief Highlights	5
A. Levels of Management	6
B. What the Supervisor Must Learn	6
C. A Definition of Supervision	6
D. Elements of the Team Concept	6
E. Principles of Organization	6
F. The Four Important Parts of Every Job	7
G. Principles of Delegation	7
H. Principles of Effective Communications	7
I. Principles of Work Improvement	7
J. Areas of Job Improvement	7
K. Seven Key Points in Making Improvements	8

	L.	Corrective Techniques for Job Improvement	8
	M.	A Planning Checklist	8
	N.	Five Characteristics of Good Directions	9
	O.	Types of Directions	9
	P.	Controls	9
	Q.	Orienting the New Employee	9
	R.	Checklist for Orienting New Employees	9
	S.	Principles of Learning	10
	T.	Causes of Poor Performance	10
	U.	Four Major Steps in On-the-Job Instructions	10
	V.	Employees Want Five Things	10
	W.	Some Don'ts in Regard to Praise	11
	X.	How to Gain Your Workers' Confidence	11
	Y.	Sources of Employee Problems	11
	Z.	The Supervisor's Key to Discipline	11
	AA.	Five Important Processes of Management	12
	BB.	When the Supervisor Fails to Plan	12
	CC.	Fourteen General Principles of Management	12
	DD.	Change	12
II.	Brief Topical Summaries		13
	A.	Who/What is the Supervisor?	13
	B.	The Sociology of Work	13
	C.	Principles and Practices of Supervision	14
	D.	Dynamic Leadership	14
	E.	Processes for Solving Problems	15
	F.	Training for Results	15
	G.	Health, Safety, and Accident Prevention	16
	H.	Equal Employment Opportunity	16
	I.	Improving Communications	16
	J.	Self-Development	17
	K.	Teaching and Training	17
		1. The Teaching Process	17
		a. Preparation	17
		b. Presentation	18
		c. Summary	18
		d. Application	18
		e. Evaluation	18
		2. Teaching Methods	18
		a. Lecture	18
		b. Discussion	18
		c. Demonstration	19
		d. Performance	19
		e. Which Method to Use	19

PHILOSOPHY, PRINCIPLES, PRACTICES, AND TECHNICS
OF
SUPERVISION, ADMINISTRATION, MANAGEMENT, AND ORGANIZATION

MEANING OF SUPERVISION

The extension of the democratic philosophy has been accompanied by an extension in the scope of supervision. Modern leaders and supervisors no longer think of supervision in the narrow sense of being confined chiefly to visiting employees, supplying materials, or rating the staff. They regard supervision as being intimately related to all the concerned agencies of society, they speak of the supervisor's function in terms of "growth," rather than the "improvement" of employees.

This modern concept of supervision may be defined as follows: Supervision is leadership and the development of leadership within groups which are cooperatively engaged in inspection, research, training, guidance, and evaluation.

THE OLD AND THE NEW SUPERVISION

TRADITIONAL
1. Inspection
2. Focused on the employee
3. Visitation
4. Random and haphazard
5. Imposed and authoritarian
6. One person usually

MODERN
1. Study and analysis
2. Focused on aims, materials, methods, supervisors, employees, environment
3. Demonstrations, intervisitation, workshops, directed reading, bulletins, etc.
4. Definitely organized and planned (scientific)
5. Cooperative and democratic
6. Many persons involved (creative)

THE EIGHT (8) BASIC PRINCIPLES OF THE NEW SUPERVISION

I. Principle of Responsibility
   Authority to act and responsibility for acting must be joined.
   A. If you give responsibility, give authority.
   B. Define employee duties clearly.
   C. Protect employees from criticism by others.
   D. Recognize the rights as well as obligations of employees.
   E. Achieve the aims of a democratic society insofar as it is possible within the area of your work.
   F. Establish a situation favorable to training and learning.
   G. Accept ultimate responsibility for everything done in your section, unit, office, division, department.
   H. Good administration and good supervision are inseparable.

II. Principle of Authority
The success of the supervisor is measured by the extent to which the power of authority is not used.
   A. Exercise simplicity and informality in supervision
   B. Use the simplest machinery of supervision
   C. If it is good for the organization as a whole, it is probably justified.
   D. Seldom be arbitrary or authoritative.
   E. Do not base your work on the power of position or of personality.
   F. Permit and encourage the free expression of opinions.

III. Principle of Self-Growth
The success of the supervisor is measured by the extent to which, and the speed with which, he is no longer needed.
   A. Base criticism on principles, not on specifics.
   B. Point out higher activities to employees.
   C. Train for self-thinking by employees to meet new situations.
   D. Stimulate initiative, self-reliance, and individual responsibility
   E. Concentrate on stimulating the growth of employees rather than on removing defects.

IV. Principle of Individual Worth
Respect for the individual is a paramount consideration in supervision.
   A. Be human and sympathetic in dealing with employees.
   B. Don't nag about things to be done.
   C. Recognize the individual differences among employees and seek opportunities to permit best expression of each personality.

V. Principle of Creative Leadership
The best supervision is that which is not apparent to the employee.
   A. Stimulate, don't drive employees to creative action.
   B. Emphasize doing good things.
   C. Encourage employees to do what they do best.
   D. Do not be too greatly concerned with details of subject or method.
   E. Do not be concerned exclusively with immediate problems and activities.
   F. Reveal higher activities and make them both desired and maximally possible.
   G. Determine procedures in the light of each situation but see that these are derived from a sound basic philosophy.
   H. Aid, inspire, and lead so as to liberate the creative spirit latent in all good employees.

VI. Principle of Success and Failure
There are no unsuccessful employees, only unsuccessful supervisors who have failed to give proper leadership.
   A. Adapt suggestions to the capacities, attitudes, and prejudices of employees.
   B. Be gradual, be progressive, be persistent.
   C. Help the employee find the general principle; have the employee apply his own problem to the general principle.
   D. Give adequate appreciation for good work and honest effort.
   E. Anticipate employee difficulties and help to prevent them.
   F. Encourage employees to do the desirable things they will do anyway.
   G. Judge your supervision by the results it secures.

VII. Principle of Science
Successful supervision is scientific, objective, and experimental. It is based on facts, not on prejudices.
- A. Be cumulative in results.
- B. Never divorce your suggestions from the goals of training.
- C. Don't be impatient of results.
- D. Keep all matters on a professional, not a personal, level.
- E. Do not be concerned exclusively with immediate problems and activities.
- F. Use objective means of determining achievement and rating where possible.

VIII. Principle of Cooperation
Supervision is a cooperative enterprise between supervisor and employee.
- A. Begin with conditions as they are.
- B. Ask opinions of all involved when formulating policies.
- C. Organization is as good as its weakest link.
- D. Let employees help to determine policies and department programs.
- E. Be approachable and accessible—physically and mentally.
- F. Develop pleasant social relationships.

WHAT IS ADMINISTRATION

Administration is concerned with providing the environment, the material facilities, and the operational procedures that will promote the maximum growth and development of supervisors and employees. (Organization is an aspect and a concomitant of administration.)

There is no sharp line of demarcation between supervision and administration; these functions are intimately interrelated and, often, overlapping. They are complementary activities.

I. Practices Commonly Classed as "Supervisory"
- A. Conducting employees' conferences
- B. Visiting sections, units, offices, divisions, departments
- C. Arranging for demonstrations
- D. Examining plans
- E. Suggesting professional reading
- F. Interpreting bulletins
- G. Recommending in-service training courses
- H. Encouraging experimentation
- I. Appraising employee morale
- J. Providing for intervisitation

II. Practices Commonly Classified as "Administrative"
- A. Management of the office
- B. Arrangement of schedules for extra duties
- C. Assignment of rooms or areas
- D. Distribution of supplies
- E. Keeping records and reports
- F. Care of audio-visual materials
- G. Keeping inventory records
- H. Checking record cards and books

I. Programming special activities
J. Checking on the attendance and punctuality of employees

III. Practices Commonly Classified as Both "Supervisory" and "Administrative"
A. Program construction
B. Testing or evaluating outcomes
C. Personnel accounting
D. Ordering instructional materials

RESPONSIBILITIES OF THE SUPERVISOR

A person employed in a supervisory capacity must constantly be able to improve his own efficiency and ability. He represent the employer to the employees and only continuous self-examination can make him a capable supervisor.

Leadership and training are the supervisor's responsibility. An efficient working unit is one in which the employees work with the supervisor. It is his job to bring out the best in his employees. He must always be relaxed, courteous, and calm in his association with his employees. Their feelings are important, and a harsh attitude does not develop the most efficient employees.

COMPETENCES OF THE SUPERVISOR

I. Complete knowledge of the duties and responsibilities of his position.
II. To be able to organize a job, plan ahead, and carry through.
III. To have self-confidence and initiative.
IV. To be able to handle the unexpected situation and make quick decisions.
V. To be able to properly train subordinates in the positions they are best suited for.
VI. To be able to keep good human relations among his subordinates.
VII. To be able to keep good human relations between his subordinates and himself and to earn their respect and trust.

THE PROFESSIONAL SUPERVISOR-EMPLOYEE RELATIONSHIP

There are two kinds of efficiency: one kind is only apparent and is produced in organizations through the exercise of mere discipline; this is but a simulation of the second, or true, efficiency which springs from spontaneous cooperation. If you are a manager, no matter how great or small your responsibility, it is your job, in the final analysis, to create and develop this involuntary cooperation among the people whom you supervise. For, no matter how powerful a combination of money, machines, and materials a company may have, this is a dead and sterile thing without a team of willing, thinking, and articulate people to guide it.

The following 21 points are presented as indicative of the exemplary basic relationship that should exist between supervisor and employee:

1. Each person wants to be liked and respected by his fellow employee and wants to be treated with consideration and respect by his superior.
2. The most competent employee will make an error. However, in a unit where good relations exist between the supervisor and his employees, tenseness and fear do not exist. Thus, errors are not hidden or covered up, and the efficiency of a unit is not impaired.

3. Subordinates resent rules, regulations, or orders that are unreasonable or unexplained.
4. Subordinates are quick to resent unfairness, harshness, injustices, and favoritism.
5. An employee will accept responsibility if he knows that he will be complimented for a job well done, and not too harshly chastised for failure; that his supervisor will check the cause of the failure, and, if it was the supervisor's fault, he will assume the blame therefore. If it was the employee's fault, his supervisor will explain the correct method or means of handling the responsibility.
6. An employee wants to receive credit for a suggestion he has made, that is used. If a suggestion cannot be used, the employee is entitled to an explanation. The supervisor should not say "no" and close the subject.
7. Fear and worry slow up a worker's ability. Poor working environment can impair his physical and mental health. A good supervisor avoids forceful methods, threats, and arguments to get a job done.
8. A forceful supervisor is able to train his employees individually and as a team, and is able to motivate them in the proper channels.
9. A mature supervisor is able to properly evaluate his subordinates and to keep them happy and satisfied.
10. A sensitive supervisor will never patronize his subordinates.
11. A worthy supervisor will respect his employees' confidences.
12. Definite and clear-cut responsibilities should be assigned to each executive.
13. Responsibility should always be coupled with corresponding authority.
14. No change should be made in the scope or responsibilities of a position without a definite understanding to that effect on the part of all persons concerned.
15. No executive or employee, occupying a single position in the organization, should be subject to definite orders from more than one source.
16. Orders should never be given to subordinates over the head of a responsible executive. Rather than do this, the officer in question should be supplanted.
17. Criticisms of subordinates should, whoever possible, be made privately, and in no case should a subordinate be criticized in the presence of executives or employees of equal or lower rank.
18. No dispute or difference between executives or employees as to authority or responsibilities should be considered too trivial for prompt and careful adjudication.
19. Promotions, wage changes, and disciplinary action should always be approved by the executive immediately superior to the one directly responsible.
20. No executive or employee should ever be required, or expected, to be at the same time an assistant to, and critic of, another.
21. Any executive whose work is subject to regular inspection should, wherever practicable, be given the assistance and facilities necessary to enable him to maintain an independent check of the quality of his work.

MINI-TEXT IN SUPERVISION, ADMINISTRATION, MANAGEMENT, AND ORGANIZATION

I. Brief Highlights

Listed concisely and sequentially are major headings and important data in the field for quick recall and review.

A. Levels of Management
Any organization of some size has several levels of management. In terms of a ladder, the levels are:

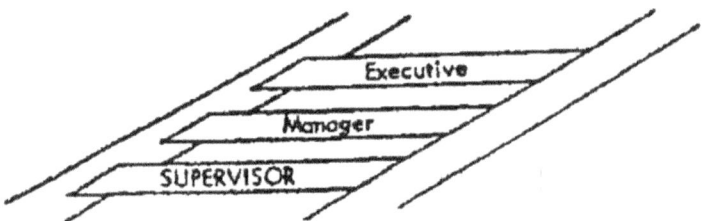

The first level is very important because it is the beginning point of management leadership.

B. What the Supervisor Must Learn
A supervisor must learn to:
1. Deal with people and their differences
2. Get the job done through people
3. Recognize the problems when they exist
4. Overcome obstacles to good performance
5. Evaluate the performance of people
6. Check his own performance in terms of accomplishment

C. A Definition of Supervisor
The term supervisor means any individual having authority, in the interests of the employer, to hire, transfer, suspend, lay-off, recall, promote, discharge, assign, reward, or discipline other employees or responsibility to direct them, or to adjust their grievances, or effectively to recommend such action, if, in connection with the foregoing, exercise of such authority is not of a merely routine or clerical nature but requires the use of independent judgment.

D. Elements of the Team Concept
What is involved in teamwork? The component parts are:
1. Members
2. A leader
3. Goals
4. Plans
5. Cooperation
6. Spirit

E. Principles of Organization
1. A team member must know what his job is.
2. Be sure that the nature and scope of a job are understood.
3. Authority and responsibility should be carefully spelled out.
4. A supervisor should be permitted to make the maximum number of decisions affecting his employees.
5. Employees should report to only one supervisor.
6. A supervisor should direct only as many employees as he can handle effectively.
7. An organization plan should be flexible.

8. Inspection and performance of work should be separate.
9. Organizational problems should receive immediate attention.
10. Assign work in line with ability and experience.

F. The Four Important Parts of Every Job
1. Inherent in every job is the *accountability* for results.
2. A second set of factors in every job is *responsibilities*.
3. Along with duties and responsibilities one must have the *authority* to act within certain limits without obtaining permission to proceed.
4. No job exists in a vacuum. The supervisor is surrounded by key *relationships*.

G. Principles of Delegation
Where work is delegated for the first time, the supervisor should think in terms of these questions:
1. Who is best qualified to do this?
2. Can an employee improve his abilities by doing this?
3. How long should an employee spend on this?
4. Are there any special problems for which he will need guidance?
5. How broad a delegation can I make?

H. Principles of Effective Communications
1. Determine the media.
2. To whom directed?
3. Identification and source authority.
4. Is communication understood?

I. Principles of Work Improvement
1. Most people usually do only the work which is assigned to them.
2. Workers are likely to fit assigned work into the time available to perform it.
3. A good workload usually stimulates output.
4. People usually do their best work when they know that results will be reviewed or inspected.
5. Employees usually feel that someone else is responsible for conditions of work, workplace layout, job methods, type of tools/equipment, and other such factors.
6. Employees are usually defensive about their job security.
7. Employees have natural resistance to change.
8. Employees can support or destroy a supervisor.
9. A supervisor usually earns the respect of his people through his personal example of diligence and efficiency.

J. Areas of Job Improvement
The areas of job improvement are quite numerous, but the most common ones which a supervisor can identify and utilize are:
1. Departmental layout
2. Flow of work
3. Workplace layout
4. Utilization of manpower
5. Work methods
6. Materials handling

       7.   Utilization
       8.   Motion economy

K. Seven Key Points in Making Improvements
1. Select the job to be improved
2. Study how it is being done now
3. Question the present method
4. Determine actions to be taken
5. Chart proposed method
6. Get approval and apply
7. Solicit worker participation

L. Corrective Techniques of Job Improvement
Specific Problems
1. Size of workload
2. Inability to meet schedules
3. Strain and fatigue
4. Improper use of men and skills
5. Waste, poor quality, unsafe conditions
6. Bottleneck conditions that hinder output
7. Poor utilization of equipment and machine
8. Efficiency and productivity of labor

General Improvement
1. Departmental layout
2. Flow of work
3. Work plan layout
4. Utilization of manpower
5. Work methods
6. Materials handling
7. Utilization of equipment
8. Motion economy

Corrective Techniques
1. Study with scale model
2. Flow chart study
3. Motion analysis
4. Comparison of units produced to standard allowance
5. Methods analysis
6. Flow chart and equipment study
7. Down time vs. running time
8. Motion analysis

M. A Planning Checklist
1. Objectives
2. Controls
3. Delegations
4. Communications
5. Resources
6. Manpower

7. Equipment
8. Supplies and materials
9. Utilization of time
10. Safety
11. Money
12. Work
13. Timing of improvements

N. Five Characteristics of Good Directions
In order to get results, directions must be:
1. Possible of accomplishment
2. Agreeable with worker interests
3. Related to mission
4. Planned and complete
5. Unmistakably clear

O. Types of Directions
1. Demands or direct orders
2. Requests
3. Suggestion or implication
4. volunteering

P. Controls
A typical listing of the overall areas in which the supervisor should establish controls might be:
1. Manpower
2. Materials
3. Quality of work
4. Quantity of work
5. Time
6. Space
7. Money
8. Methods

Q. Orienting the New Employee
1. Prepare for him
2. Welcome the new employee
3. Orientation for the job
4. Follow-up

R. Checklist for Orienting New Employees   Yes   No
1. Do you appreciate the feelings of new employees
   when they first report for work?   ___   ___
2. Are you aware of the fact that the new employee must
   make a big adjustment to his job?   ___   ___
3. Have you given him good reasons for liking the job and
   the organization?   ___   ___
4. Have you prepared for his first day on the job?   ___   ___
5. Did you welcome him cordially and make him feel needed?   ___   ___

	Yes	No
6. Did you establish rapport with him so that he feels free to talk and discuss matters with you?	___	___
7. Did you explain his job to him and his relationship to you?	___	___
8. Does he know that his work will be evaluated periodically on a basis that is fair and objective?	___	___
9. Did you introduce him to his fellow workers in such a way that they are likely to accept him?	___	___
10. Does he know what employee benefits he will receive?	___	___
11. Does he understand the importance of being on the job and what to do if he must leave his duty station?	___	___
12. Has he been impressed with the importance of accident prevention and safe practice?	___	___
13. Does he generally know his way around the department?	___	___
14. Is he under the guidance of a sponsor who will teach the right way of doing things?	___	___
15. Do you plan to follow-up so that he will continue to adjust successfully to his job?	___	___

S. Principles of Learning
   1. Motivation
   2. Demonstration or explanation
   3. Practice

T. Causes of Poor Performance
   1. Improper training for job
   2. Wrong tools
   3. Inadequate directions
   4. Lack of supervisory follow-up
   5. Poor communications
   6. Lack of standards of performance
   7. Wrong work habits
   8. Low morale
   9. Other

U. Four Major Steps in On-The-Job Instruction
   1. Prepare the worker
   2. Present the operation
   3. Tryout performance
   4. Follow-up

V. Employees Want Five Things
   1. Security
   2. Opportunity
   3. Recognition
   4. Inclusion
   5. Expression

W. Some Don'ts in Regard to Praise
1. Don't praise a person for something he hasn't done.
2. Don't praise a person unless you can be sincere.
3. Don't be sparing in praise just because your superior withholds it from you.
4. Don't let too much time elapse between good performance and recognition of it

X. How to Gain Your Workers' Confidence
Methods of developing confidence include such things as:
1. Knowing the interests, habits, hobbies of employees
2. Admitting your own inadequacies
3. Sharing and telling of confidence in others
4. Supporting people when they are in trouble
5. Delegating matters that can be well handled
6. Being frank and straightforward about problems and working conditions
7. Encouraging others to bring their problems to you
8. Taking action on problems which impede worker progress

Y. Sources of Employee Problems
On-the-job causes might be such things as:
1. A feeling that favoritism is exercised in assignments
2. Assignment of overtime
3. An undue amount of supervision
4. Changing methods or systems
5. Stealing of ideas or trade secrets
6. Lack of interest in job
7. Threat of reduction in force
8. Ignorance or lack of communications
9. Poor equipment
10. Lack of knowing how supervisor feels toward employee
11. Shift assignments

Off-the-job problems might have to do with:
1. Health
2. Finances
3. Housing
4. Family

Z. The Supervisor's Key to Discipline
There are several key points about discipline which the supervisor should keep in mind:
1. Job discipline is one of the disciplines of life and is directed by the supervisor.
2. It is more important to correct an employee fault than to fix blame for it.
3. Employee performance is affected by problems both on the job and off.
4. Sudden or abrupt changes in behavior can be indications of important employee problems.
5. Problems should be dealt with as soon as possible after they are identified.
6. The attitude of the supervisor may have more to do with solving problems than the techniques of problem solving.
7. Correction of employee behavior should be resorted to only after the supervisor is sure that training or counseling will not be helpful.

8. Be sure to document your disciplinary actions.
9. Make sure that you are disciplining on the basis of facts rather than personal feelings.
10. Take each disciplinary step in order, being careful not to make snap judgments, or decisions based on impatience.

AA. Five Important Processes of Management
1. Planning
2. Organizing
3. Scheduling
4. Controlling
5. Motivating

BB. When the Supervisor Fails to Plan
1. Supervisor creates impression of not knowing his job
2. May lead to excessive overtime
3. Job runs itself—supervisor lacks control
4. Deadlines and appointments missed
5. Parts of the work go undone
6. Work interrupted by emergencies
7. Sets a bad example
8. Uneven workload creates peaks and valleys
9. Too much time on minor details at expense of more important tasks

CC. Fourteen General Principles of Management
1. Division of work
2. Authority and responsibility
3. Discipline
4. Unity of command
5. Unity of direction
6. Subordination of individual interest to general interest
7. Remuneration of personnel
8. Centralization
9. Scalar chain
10. Order
11. Equity
12. Stability of tenure of personnel
13. Initiative
14. Esprit de corps

DD. Change

Bringing about change is perhaps attempted more often, and yet less well understood, than anything else the supervisor does. How do people generally react to change? (People tend to resist change that is imposed upon them by other individuals or circumstances.

Change is characteristic of every situation. It is a part of every real endeavor where the efforts of people are concerned.

1. Why do people resist change?
   People may resist change because of:
   a. Fear of the unknown
   b. Implied criticism
   c. Unpleasant experiences in the past
   d. Fear of loss of status
   e. Threat to the ego
   f. Fear of loss of economic stability

2. How can we best overcome the resistance to change?
   In initiating change, take these steps:
   a. Get ready to sell
   b. Identify sources of help
   c. Anticipate objections
   d. Sell benefits
   e. Listen in depth
   f. Follow up

II. Brief Topical Summaries

   A. Who/What is the Supervisor?
      1. The supervisor is often called the "highest level employee and the lowest level manager."
      2. A supervisor is a member of both management and the work group. He acts as a bridge between the two.
      3. Most problems in supervision are in the area of human relations, or people problems.
      4. Employees expect: Respect, opportunity to learn and to advance, and a sense of belonging, and so forth.
      5. Supervisors are responsible for directing people and organizing work. Planning is of paramount importance.
      6. A position description is a set of duties and responsibilities inherent to a given position.
      7. It is important to keep the position description up-to-date and to provide each employee with his own copy.

   B. The Sociology of Work
      1. People are alike in many ways; however, each individual is unique.
      2. The supervisor is challenged in getting to know employee differences. Acquiring skills in evaluating individuals is an asset.
      3. Maintaining meaningful working relationships in the organization is of great importance.
      4. The supervisor has an obligation to help individuals to develop to their fullest potential.
      5. Job rotation on a planned basis helps to build versatility and to maintain interest and enthusiasm in work groups.
      6. Cross training (job rotation) provides backup skills.

7. The supervisor can help reduce tension by maintaining a sense of humor, providing guidance to employees, and by making reasonable and timely decisions. Employees respond favorably to working under reasonably predictable circumstances.
8. Change is characteristic of all managerial behavior. The supervisor must adjust to changes in procedures, new methods, technological changes, and to a number of new and sometimes challenging situations.
9. To overcome the natural tendency for people to resist change, the supervisor should become more skillful in initiating change.

C. Principles and Practices of Supervision
1. Employees should be required to answer to only one superior.
2. A supervisor can effectively direct only a limited number of employees, depending upon the complexity, variety, and proximity of the jobs involved.
3. The organizational chart presents the organization in graphic form. It reflects lines of authority and responsibility as well as interrelationships of units within the organization.
4. Distribution of work can be improved through an analysis using the "Work Distribution Chart."
5. The "Work Distribution Chart" reflects the division of work within a unit in understandable form.
6. When related tasks are given to an employee, he has a better chance of increasing his skills through training.
7. The individual who is given the responsibility for tasks must also be given the appropriate authority to insure adequate results.
8. The supervisor should delegate repetitive, routine work. Preparation of recurring reports, maintaining leave and attendance records are some examples.
9. Good discipline is essential to good task performance. Discipline is reflected in the actions of employees on the job in the absence of supervision.
10. Disciplinary action may have to be taken when the positive aspects of discipline have failed. Reprimand, warning, and suspension are examples of disciplinary action.
11. If a situation calls for a reprimand, be sure it is deserved and remember it is to be done in private.

D. Dynamic Leadership
1. A style is a personal method or manner of exerting influence.
2. Authoritarian leaders often see themselves as the source of power and authority.
3. The democratic leader often perceives the group as the source of authority and power.
4. Supervisors tend to do better when using the pattern of leadership that is most natural for them.
5. Social scientists suggest that the effective supervisor use the leadership style that best fits the problem or circumstances involved.
6. All four styles—telling, selling, consulting, joining—have their place. Using one does not preclude using the other at another time.

7. The theory X point of view assumes that the average person dislikes work, will avoid it whenever possible, and must be coerced to achieve organizational objectives.
8. The theory Y point of view assumes that the average person considers work to be a natural as play, and, when the individual is committed, he requires little supervision or direction to accomplish desired objectives.
9. The leader's basic assumptions concerning human behavior and human nature affect his actions, decisions, and other managerial practices.
10. Dissatisfaction among employees is often present, but difficult to isolate. The supervisor should seek to weaken dissatisfaction by keeping promises, being sincere and considerate, keeping employees informed, and so forth.
11. Constructive suggestions should be encouraged during the natural progress of the work.

E. Processes for Solving Problems
1. People find their daily tasks more meaningful and satisfying when they can improve them.
2. The causes of problems, or the key factors, are often hidden in the background. Ability to solve problems often involves the ability to isolate them from their backgrounds. There is some substance to the cliché that some persons "can't see the forest for the trees."
3. New procedures are often developed from old ones. Problems should be broken down into manageable parts. New ideas can be adapted from old one.
4. People think differently in problem-solving situations. Using a logical, patterned approach is often useful. One approach found to be useful includes these steps:
   a. Define the problem
   b. Establish objectives
   c. Get the facts
   d. Weigh and decide
   e. Take action
   f. Evaluate action

F. Training for Results
1. Participants respond best when they feel training is important to them.
2. The supervisor has responsibility for the training and development of those who report to him.
3. When training is delegated to others, great care must be exercised to insure the trainer has knowledge, aptitude, and interest for his work as a trainer.
4. Training (learning) of some type goes on continually. The most successful supervisor makes certain the learning contributes in a productive manner to operational goals.
5. New employees are particularly susceptible to training. Older employees facing new job situations require specific training, as well as having need for development and growth opportunities.
6. Training needs require continuous monitoring.
7. The training officer of an agency is a professional with a responsibility to assist supervisors in solving training problems.

8. Many of the self-development steps important to the supervisor's own growth are equally important to the development of peers and subordinates. Knowledge of these is important when the supervisor consults with others on development and growth opportunities.

G. Health, Safety, and Accident Prevention
1. Management-minded supervisors take appropriate measures to assist employees in maintaining health and in assuring safe practices in the work environment.
2. Effective safety training and practices help to avoid injury and accidents.
3. Safety should be a management goal. All infractions of safety which are observed should be corrected without exception.
4. Employees' safety attitude, training and instruction, provision of safe tools and equipment, supervision, and leadership are considered highly important factors which contribute to safety and which can be influenced directly by supervisors.
5. When accidents do occur, they should be investigated promptly for very important reasons, including the fact that information which is gained can be used to prevent accidents in the future.

H. Equal Employment Opportunity
1. The supervisor should endeavor to treat all employees fairly, without regard to religion, race, sex, or national origin.
2. Groups tend to reflect the attitude of the leader. Prejudice can be detected even in very subtle form. Supervisors must strive to create a feeling of mutual respect and confidence in every employee.
3. Complete utilization of all human resources is a national goal. Equitable consideration should be accorded women in the work force, minority-group members, the physically and mentally handicapped, and the older employee. The important question is: "Who can do the job?"
4. Training opportunities, recognition for performance, overtime assignments, promotional opportunities, and all other personnel actions are to be handled on an equitable basis.

I. Improving Communications
1. Communications is achieving understanding between the sender and the receiver of a message. It also means sharing information—the creation of understanding.
2. Communication is basic to all human activity. Words are means of conveying meanings; however, real meanings are in people.
3. There are very practical differences in the effectiveness of one-way, impersonal, and two-way communications. Words spoken face-to-face are better understood. Telephone conversations are effective, but lack the rapport of person-to-person exchanges. The whole person communicates.
4. Cooperation and communication in an organization go hand in hand. When there is a mutual respect between people, spelling out rules and procedures for communicating is unnecessary.
5. There are several barriers to effective communications. These include failure to listen with respect and understanding, lack of skill in feedback, and misinterpreting the meanings of words used by the speaker. It is also common

practice to listen to what we want to hear, and tune out things we do not want to hear.
6. Communication is management's chief problem. The supervisor should accept the challenge to communicate more effectively and to improve interagency and intra-agency communications.
7. The supervisor may often plan for and conduct meetings. The planning phase is critical and may determine the success or the failure of a meeting.
8. Speaking before groups usually requires extra effort. Stage fright may never disappear completely, but it can be controlled.

J. Self-Development
1. Every employee is responsible for his own self-development.
2. Toastmaster and toastmistress clubs offer opportunities to improve skills in oral communications.
3. Planning for one's own self-development is of vital importance. Supervisors know their own strengths and limitations better than anyone else.
4. Many opportunities are open to aid the supervisor in his developmental efforts, including job assignments; training opportunities, both governmental and non-governmental—to include universities and professional conferences and seminars.
5. Programmed instruction offers a means of studying at one's own rate.
6. Where difficulties may arise from a supervisor's being away from his work for training, he may participate in televised home study or correspondence courses to meet his self-development needs.

K. Teaching and Training
1. The Teaching Process
Teaching is encouraging and guiding the learning activities of students toward established goals. In most cases this process consists of five steps: preparation, presentation, summarization, evaluation, and application.

  a. Preparation
  Preparation is two-fold in nature; that of the supervisor and the employee. Preparation by the supervisor is absolutely essential to success. He must know what, when, where, how, and whom he will teach. Some of the factors that should be considered are:
  1) The objectives
  2) The materials needed
  3) The methods to be used
  4) Employee participation
  5) Employee interest
  6) Training aids
  7) Evaluation
  8) Summarization

  Employee preparation consists in preparing the employee to receive the material. Probably the most important single factor in the preparation of the employee is arousing and maintaining his interest. He must know the objectives of the training, why he is there, how the material can be used, and its importance to him.

18

b. Presentation
In presentation, have a carefully designed plan and follow it. The plan should be accurate and complete, yet flexible enough to meet situations as they arise. The method of presentation will be determined by the particular situation and objectives.

c. Summary
A summary should be made at the end of every training unit and program. In addition, there may be internal summaries depending on the nature of the material being taught. The important thing is that the trainee must always be able to understand how each part of the new material relates to the whole.

d. Application
The supervisor must arrange work so the employee will be given a chance to apply new knowledge or skills while the material is still clear in his mind and interest is high. The trainee does not really know whether he has learned the material until he has been given a chance to apply it. If the material is not applied, it loses most of its value.

e. Evaluation
The purpose of all training is to promote learning. To determine whether the training has been a success or failure, the supervisor must evaluate this learning.
In the broadest sense, evaluation includes all the devices, methods, skills, and techniques used by the supervisor to keep himself and the employees informed as to their progress toward the objectives they are pursuing. The extent to which the employee has mastered the knowledge, skills, and abilities, or changed his attitudes, as determined by the program objectives, is the extent to which instruction has succeeded or failed.
Evaluation should not be confined to the end of the lesson, day, or program but should be used continuously. We shall note later the way this relates to the rest of the teaching process.

2. Teaching Methods
A teaching method is a pattern of identifiable student and instructor activity used in presenting training material.
All supervisors are faced with the problem of deciding which method should be used at a given time.

a. Lecture
The lecture is direct oral presentation of material by the supervisor. The present trend is to place less emphasis on the trainer's activity and more on that of the trainee.

b. Discussion
Teaching by discussion or conference involves using questions and other techniques to arouse interest and focus attention upon certain areas, and by doing so creating a learning situation. This can be one of the most

valuable methods because it gives the employees an opportunity to express their ideas and pool their knowledge.

c. Demonstration
The demonstration is used to teach how something works or how to do something. It can be used to show a principle or what the results of a series of actions will be. A well-staged demonstration is particularly effective because it shows proper methods of performance in a realistic manner.

d. Performance
Performance is one of the most fundamental of all learning techniques or teaching methods. The trainee may be able to tell how a specific operation should be performed but he cannot be sure he knows how to perform the operation until he has done so.
As with all methods, there are certain advantages and disadvantages to each method.

e. Which Method to Use
Moreover, there are other methods and techniques of teaching. It is difficult to use any method without other methods entering into it. In any learning situation, a combination of methods is usually more effective than any one method alone.

Finally, evaluation must be integrated into the other aspects of the teaching-learning process.

It must be used in the motivation of the trainees; it must be used to assist in developing understanding during the training; and it must be related to employee application of the results of training.

This is distinctly the role of the supervisor.

www.ingramcontent.com/pod-product-compliance
Lightning Source LLC
Chambersburg PA
CBHW081813300426
44116CB00014B/2342